T0356382

KINDA KOREAN

STORIES FROM AN AMERICAN LIFE

JOAN SUNG

SHE WRITES PRESS

Copyright © 2025 Joan Sung

All rights reserved. No part of this publication may be reproduced, distributed, or transmitted in any form or by any means, including photocopying, recording, digital scanning, or other electronic or mechanical methods, without the prior written permission of the publisher, except in the case of brief quotations embodied in critical reviews and certain other noncommercial uses permitted by copyright law. For permission requests, please address She Writes Press.

Published 2025
Printed in the United States of America
Print ISBN: 978-1-64742-842-6
E-ISBN: 978-1-64742-843-3
Library of Congress Control Number: 2024918955

For information, address:
She Writes Press
1569 Solano Ave #546
Berkeley, CA 94707

Interior Design by Andrea Reider

She Writes Press is a division of SparkPoint Studio, LLC.

Company and/or product names that are trade names, logos, trademarks, and/or registered trademarks of third parties are the property of their respective owners and are used in this book for purposes of identification and information only under the Fair Use Doctrine.

NO AI TRAINING: Without in any way limiting the author's [and publisher's] exclusive rights under copyright, any use of this publication to "train" generative artificial intelligence (AI) technologies to generate text is expressly prohibited. The author reserves all rights to license uses of this work for generative AI training and development of machine learning language models.

Names and identifying characteristics have been changed to protect the privacy of certain individuals.

To all the Asian American women who ever felt alone.
I am here with you.

Umma: Meeyahn-heh-yoh.

TABLE OF CONTENTS

I looked at her little white dog, who was sitting up in a stroller. He looked at me imploringly for an escape route as I stared at the ridiculous ponytail that sat between his ears. I gazed around the crystal shop and wondered how I, a proud cynic, came to be here. The oracle's bracelets clacked together rhythmically as she moved her hands over me, perhaps trying to read my energy. Her eyes were closed, and she was nodding. I uneasily adjusted in my chair.

My eyes narrowed in skepticism. The woman was beautiful, no doubt—she wore thick acrylic glasses, and her shaved head glinted as the light caught her silver hairs. She continued to nod, almost as if listening to my inner voice rambling on. Her ebony skin was smooth with the exception of the few deeply sketched laugh lines on her cheeks. She tilted one ear toward me and leaned in, an action that still made me nervous given that, this time the previous year, we were all wearing masks and told to stay six feet apart from one another. I took a deep breath, eager to gauge the validity of what she had to say.

A friend once told me that oracles are in the business of holding a mirror up to you: What do their words mean to *you*? The significance is not exactly what they say but how you internalize what they say: you hear what you need to in that moment. And it was this insight that sparked my curiosity. I just had to see for myself if an oracle could help me, as I had spent the last year experiencing racial fatigue and trauma amid the rise in anti-Asian hate crimes across the United States. I needed guidance around understanding my place in a society that constantly labeled me as a Perpetual Foreigner.

"Okay," the oracle said abruptly, and sat back in her chair. I raised my eyebrows in expectation. "Before we begin, we need to acknowledge something." I held my breath. To my surprise, her face broke into a wide smile.

"You," she started, "have a beautiful life." I felt startled. But when I reflected briefly, images of my loving husband and adoring son bloomed in my mind. Automatically, I grinned.

"I do." I nodded in agreement. "I really do," I said, feeling my eyes swell.

But she leaned in again, this time her voice dropping to a whisper. "But you have some healing to do."

My grin waned. I immediately thought of my strained relationship with my tiger mom.

"You need to address your . . . *intergenerational trauma*," she said gently.

I was taken aback at the specificity. *How did she know?* I suppose she could have thrown anything out there in hopes that it would stick, like spaghetti thrown at a cupboard. If this was a hoax, why not mention something broader? Like "pain"? To me, "intergenerational trauma" was too specific to be a coincidence. Especially given that I had learned that year, at thirty-five years old, how my parents' immigrant trauma had manifested in me by means of panic attacks, anxiety, and depression.

But exactly how would I go about healing? How would any of us Asian Americans who'd experienced trauma with immigrant parents heal? How, when we're still unsure of our own racial identity and what it means to be Asian in America?

My thoughts turned to an Asian student I once knew when I was a classroom teacher. She wanted to talk to me over Zoom during the height of the COVID-19 pandemic, before vaccines were developed, before we were sure of the effectiveness of masks—when we thought a hug was a death sentence for our elders. This was a time when we Asian Americans were terrified to cough in public for fear of people persecuting us for bringing the virus. And I say "we" because no one could tell the difference between us Filipinos, Chinese, Japanese, Koreans—so many of us . . . leaving us all to be targets of random, senseless hate crimes.

"Why is this happening to us?" the student asked me, looking for answers from one of the few Asian teachers at her school.

"I don't know . . . I don't know," I muttered at the time. *But didn't I know?* Was it surprising that we are constantly victims of racism but told we are not, because America thinks Asians are high performing? How long have I known that Asian Americans are targets of oppression, racism, and discrimination? How can I even answer that without being able to define my own cultural identity? After all, I didn't know how to reckon a lifetime of being othered, feeling like an outsider because I was too white to be accepted by my own but too Asian for white Americans.

To find the answer to the student's question, I had to start at the beginning—*my* beginning. As the student waited for my answer on Zoom, she looked at me expectantly.

But where do I even begin?

KOREANS EAT DOGS

"**D**o Koreans really eat dogs?" a boy in my class asked me on the playground. It was a frigid winter afternoon in Seattle, Washington, and his breath puffed toward me in an urgent sort of way. He was blond and about my age, eight years old. He looked like most of the kids at my school, but he didn't look like me: I had black hair and black eyes. I was told by my classmates that the word "brunette" was reserved for white girls and boys, and black eyes made me feel as though I resembled a demon.

The boy's blue eyes looked at me alarmingly through wide-rimmed glasses. If not for the glasses, I would've jabbed a finger in his eye for the way he gawked at me, fascinated but repulsed. It was announced that morning that our class was having a potluck, and he was afraid I was going to pick off our neighborhood strays like the Son of Sam of dogs. And he wanted reassurance that I wouldn't feed him somebody's beloved family pet in a simmering Crock-Pot stew.

But this wasn't the first time I'd been asked this question about whether Koreans ate dogs. And yet, for some reason, I didn't know how to respond because I knew the answer was kind of yes, but not in the way he thought. I rehearsed a few answers quickly in my head. *My mom said that's rude to think all Koreans do . . . My dad said Korea used to be really poor . . . People had to survive—some people didn't have a choice . . .*

1

"People only did that a long time ago when they really had to," I answered lamely. My words fell flat on their face and shattered when they hit the frozen pavement.

My thoughts turned to my father. When he was a child, he fell hopelessly ill after going without food for several days. A doctor visited the family at home and told my grandparents that their son had little time to live unless they could find him something to eat. At the time, my father had a dog he cared for. Given that they were at the edge of impoverishment, my grandparents knew what they had to do. Unbeknownst to my father, they killed and cooked his dog and fed it to him. My father eventually put two and two together when he called out for his dog to no avail.

So . . . do Koreans eat dogs? *Yes,* I thought, feeling as though I had to pick one answer. *I guess they do.*

I didn't understand why kids had these assumptions about me or where these beliefs came from. I just knew that the moment I stepped foot into a space, people claimed to know things about me based on how I looked. And since my parents were immigrants and also experiencing these things, they were unable to give me any support in navigating what was happening to us. And without my parents' support, I was just left feeling . . . confused. The only guidance my mother offered was to stick my chin up and ignore negative comments. But that didn't help me make sense of it all. *Why me?* I was left wondering. *Of all kids, why does this keep happening to me? Why am I always treated like I'm not one of the other kids?*

On the playground, I stared at the boy who was somewhat satisfied with my answer and now wandering away from me. *Why me . . . ? Why me?* It was then that I came to the one inescapable conclusion: *I must be the wrong kind of different.*

TIGER MOM

"Umma . . . do you love me?" I asked for the millionth time. I was around nine years old. She was quietly singing hymns in Korean as I huddled next to the metal space heater on the floor for warmth. My brother, Chris, five years my senior, was at basketball practice. I was watching my mother as she sang, her singing a familiar sound in our house. She could usually be found in the evenings sitting on the couch, reading her Bible under a lamp. Tonight was no different. I looked at her tan, rounded face, her cheeks sprinkled with sunspots. Her pixie haircut emphasized her longer locks that cascaded in gentle waves across her forehead, the waves a residual result of an old, aggressive perm. Her petite body was stiffly upright. Her almond-shaped eyes and tattooed eyebrows were framed by her gold bifocals, which glinted in the lamplight. Her eyes were peering down at the pages, narrowing in concentration.

Without looking up from her Bible, she responded. "Stupid question."

I looked down at my hands, yearning to hear the words, just once. The words that would reassure my insecurity. The words that would cancel out the beatings that would come every time I fell short of being the perfect, obedient Korean daughter. I thought of the times I would cry after being hit with whatever might be at arm's reach: a flyswatter, a shoe, a wooden rod that my mother would use to wedge in the windowsill because we lived in an unsafe neighborhood. I would cry, and she would say sternly: "*Tteook!* Why you crying? You think you did something right?"

Her logic was something I grappled with, struggled to understand. What she meant by her stern response was: *Why are you behaving as though I am doing an injustice to you? Do you think you are in the right?* The more I cried, the angrier she would become. She would yell, "*Tteook!*"—*Suck it up!*—leaving me no option but to run to my bedroom and use a pillow to muffle my sobs.

But why would a parent lay a hand on their child if they loved them? Corporal punishment was one thing, but I knew that this was something different: my mother was taking her anger out on me. Her beatings were unhinged and uncontrolled. "*Nah-chakkeh!*" I would frequently whimper. *I'm a good girl.* After years of this, my sadness eventually morphed into rage—scarlet-hot rage. And the rage would stay, blossoming and filling out every crevice of my being. As I grew older, I would become indignant. I'd take my beating with my chin up, then retreat into my room, carefully examining my legs for permanent scars or bruises so I could call the police on my mother for child abuse. Unfortunately, that day never came. But the resentment arrived and stayed to accompany my rage.

When I was around seven years old, I spilled red juice on our new carpet. I knew what was coming. I immediately turned and ran into the bathroom to escape. But she caught up to me. And once she did, she swiftly kicked me in the stomach, sending me careening into the bathtub. It would be moments like these that I would clutch onto as I got older, feeding my desire to escape my mother like kindling trying to escape a fire.

My mother's love was the roof over our heads. My mother's love was cooking. My mother's love was cleaning. My mother's love was not, however, the one thing I had wanted from her. As I was sitting with my mother in the living room, I was still waiting for the words she held back. The words she held for ransom. I studied her profile, outlined by the living room lamp, as she sat on the couch reading her Bible.

My mother finally looked up and waved me over to where she was sitting. Was this it? Was this the moment I had been waiting for? Longing for affection, I obediently crawled onto the couch next to her. I was surprised when she handed me a glimmering pair of tweezers. Under the living room lamp, I spent the remainder of my waking minutes plucking out her grays, one at a time. Then off to bed.

REPRESENTATION MATTERS

The next morning, I was lying on the floor on my belly, my elbow propping up my hand, which was cradling my face, while my other hand flipped through a JCPenney catalog. I loved seeing what was in style, especially because I knew I could never own such trendy clothes. I gazed upon pages and pages of boys and girls posing. I noted that they were all either white or Black, but nonetheless looking confident and comfortable in their own skin. And here I was, wearing a cheesy white floral turtleneck and faded overalls my mother had obtained from the church bazaar. I hopelessly tugged at the ends of my bowl cut that my mother insisted on cutting for me because we couldn't afford a real haircut. I tugged and tugged, hoping my hair would magically grow out of my head, like the doll's hair you could lengthen just by yanking on it.

I pushed myself off of the ground and walked into the bathroom to look in the mirror. What I saw in the reflection was not what I saw represented in the catalog. I despised the shape of my eyes. They were too small, and they were missing the crease on the eyelid, *sang-gah-pool*. Even my tae kwon do instructor recently flew to Korea and got his eyes surgically enhanced to have the coveted crease. And I knew he had done this because, after he was absent for a week, he returned but wore his sunglasses indoors. In a daring move, I stepped to his side to take a peek behind his glasses and could see stitches poking out of his eyelids like barbed wire.

My eyes continued to roam over my face in the mirror. My nose . . . I hated the shape of my nose. I would kill for a button nose instead of the slightly flattened, wide nose I was given. I reached up and touched my face. *I wish I was white*, I thought miserably.

"Girls use Scotch tape to make *sang-gah-pool*," my mother told me one day after I had complained again that I was the only one in the family who wasn't born with *sang-gah-pool*. I was tired of the churchgoers cooing over how handsome my brother, Chris, was, how round and beautiful his eyes were, and how strange it was that I looked so different from him and how no one suspected we were related at first.

"If it really bother you, do this." My mother dragged a fingernail across her eyelid. "Then put Scotch tape on eyelid when fold appear. One day, it maybe stay. Some girls do this to get *sang-gah-pool*."

I took a roll of Scotch tape into the bathroom and did exactly what I was instructed to do in front of the mirror. As soon as the fold appeared, I quickly taped my eyes. I walked around with Scotch tape on my eyelids every day for a month. To my dismay, the creases never stayed.

And why would they? Even my physical appearance was evidence that, no matter how much effort I put forth, no matter that I came from my mother's gene pool, I was damned to never be my mother's daughter.

MY JEWEL

After my mother gave birth to Chris and me in Los Angeles, my parents moved us to the Seattle area. And in Seattle, my mother found a local Korean Presbyterian church to throw herself into. She had latched onto the community of all-Korean people, feeling less out of place in her life in America. Growing up, I was heavily invested in the church choir. In fourth grade, all the church choir girls were invited to a sleepover at the Korean church director's house, which was a huge deal because I was never invited to events with these girls—the popular girls. The problem was that I knew what my mother's response would be even before I asked if I could go. I wasn't allowed to sleep over. Ever.

"Korean girls don't sleep over!" she argued.

"Umma, we're American! This is the American way!" I exclaimed.

"You are *Korean*! I am *Korean*! It is Korea in this house!" she shot back. Like many other moments before this, I felt torn between the demands of two worlds. I felt too Asian in my American community, yet too American living in my own house. It was a clashing of the worlds, and I struggled to reconcile the two identities. My tiger mom was, once again, tightening her grip on me, and I didn't know how to escape.

Over the question of the sleepover, my mother stood her ground. She explained that when girls sleep over at other people's houses, where they are not safe, they return pregnant. The implication was that girls would sneak out to have sex with boys. It didn't matter how young I was; her forbidding me to sleep over was a matter of building the good habit of protecting my virtue. My brother, on the other hand, had free rein to sleep over at friends' houses whenever and wherever he pleased. Boys, according to my mother, are treated differently because they are not as fragile and need less protection.

Later that year, I sat on the toilet and stared at the pattern on the linoleum floor. I tried to make out shapes, like I did when I lay on my back in the grass to make out the shapes of passing clouds. I could see a giraffe. Or maybe the profile of a long-necked woman. I looked down at my feet and then saw the bright, crimson spot on my underwear. My gasp caught in my throat.

"*Ummahhh!*" I screamed. "*Ummahhhhhhh!*" My mother almost knocked down the bathroom door. She looked down at my underwear and gasped.

"Oh, you a woman now!"

"Umma!" I started crying. "I'm only in fourth grade!" I felt as though I had lurched forward in time, but I wasn't ready. I just wanted to hunker down on my bed with my stuffed animals. She was rummaging under the bathroom sink now, and when she found what she was looking for, she held it up triumphantly. It looked like a bulky, folded-up diaper. After she helped me clean up and showed me how to attach the pad to my fresh pair of underwear, she sat me down on the toilet. She sat on the edge of the bathtub.

"Joan, all women have . . . a jewel," she began.

What?

"If jewel have crack, it lose value. It less expensive. No one want anymore. Make sense?"

No. But I nodded.

"Okay." She smiled. "You must protect your jewel."

"Okay, Umma."

She looked pleased. When I walked out of the bathroom, Chris was lingering in the hallway. I didn't know how much he'd heard.

"What was that about?" he asked.

"I don't know . . ." I frowned. *Were we all born with gems in our vaginas? Couldn't we pawn them off and get a nicer house?* I wondered. I stared at my brother and wondered if he had a penis jewel and how much money that was worth. I felt like a walking jackpot. I pondered why our whole family didn't pool together our treasures for a more acceptable lifestyle. But my brother was so selfish, I doubted he would consider sharing his cut.

Chris and I had a typical, healthy love-hate relationship at this time. Frequently, we would sit in the back seat of our old, beat-up Mercedes-Benz, bickering while my mother drove us to one church event after another. The interior of the car was heavily stained, and the fabric on the ceiling was caved in and drooping down into the cabin, where it was held up only by safety pins.

On our way to another Korean Bible study, my mother bought us candy for the car ride, two full-size candies each—a luxury. The thing was, she bought four *different* kinds of candy. I got a pack of Starburst. Meticulously, I ate all of my least favorite flavors first in order to save the best for last. And my brother watched and waited until I was done with the less desirable flavors, then promptly protested to my mother that I wasn't sharing.

"You must share!" my mother called out from the driver's seat, her eyes glowering in the rearview mirror at me. I looked down at my lap, the best flavors left: red and pink. And slowly, I dropped half of my spoils into my brother's outreached hands, the smugness smeared across his face.

We arrived at the house that was hosting Korean Bible study for the moms at church. I gaped at the white, two-story home with the perfectly manicured green lawn. As we entered the foyer, I realized by the shoes in the entryway that a few of the daughters must have come to play with the host's daughter, Sandy. Sandy was arguably the most popular girl in our church. She was a few years older than me, so she was automatically cool but with merit: the fact that she lived in this two-story house made her untouchable. To me, a house with stairs was an indication of great wealth. Sandy wandered toward us to help her mother greet their guests and wore a Tommy Hilfiger crop top accessorized with a disinterested expression. She smacked her bubble gum and twirled her highlighted hair around one polished finger. I was certain by her layers and curtain bangs that Sandy's mother didn't cut her hair. I looked at her in envy.

The mothers went into the living room while my brother went to the backyard to look for Sandy's older brother. As soon as I removed my shoes, another church girl, Crystal, came downstairs to see who'd arrived. When she saw me, she immediately looked disappointed. Crystal was the pastor's daughter and had her ears pierced in the first grade. She was also known at the church for having gorgeous, round eyes complete with *sang-gah-pool*. Sandy sighed in boredom.

"C'mon, guys . . . let's go to the kitchen."

I obediently followed them down the hall and tried not to look too interested when the two girls began to whisper to each other. I wasn't surprised, as they frequently laughed at my clothes, which my mother purchased from the church bazaar; I was usually wearing the clothes that the church girls had discarded, and they never let me forget it.

"Soooo, Joan," Sandy said in a businesslike manner. I perked up, surprised that she'd addressed me and me alone. Generally, when she spoke to me, she acted as though she were addressing an audience—talking to no one in particular. I glanced at Crystal to assess her reaction. Crystal was looking away, avoiding my eyes.

"I heard you like candy, right?" Sandy asked coyly.

"Yes . . ." I said slowly, in disbelief that she was being so nice.

"I got this solid white-chocolate Easter bunny this year, and I've been saving it for something special. They're super hard to find."

I nodded my head, engrossed in every word.

"It's just in that pantry. Will you go get it for us? Please?" The last word she spoke lifted like the end of an ill-tempered cat's tail.

When I walked into the pantry, which was closer to the size of a small bedroom, Sandy immediately slammed the door and shut off the lights. My hand reached out to jiggle the doorknob, which was already locked. I could hear giggles erupting on the other side of the door. I began banging on it.

"Let me out!" I pleaded. I gently placed my ear to the door but could no longer hear the girls. It was silent. They had left me there. I sank to the floor of the pantry and began to cry.

The reality was these girls and I didn't live in the same America. Their America offered them infinite opportunity. My America was a constant parade of all the things I could never have. My America stripped my parents of dignity but simultaneously promised them limitless opportunity that would never be feasible. These girls' parents were rich businesspeople or had other white-collar jobs, what I thought of as "respectful" jobs. I hated it when the church kids asked me what my parents did for a living, not wanting to reveal that my father worked in a grocery store and my mother didn't work. Over the years, my father brought me home trinkets—toys, jewelry, little objects that mystified us because we didn't always know what they were. One night, I heard my mother scolding my father for bringing home nasty garbage to his daughter. I then realized for the first time that he was bringing home things that other people threw out, and items from the lost and found at work. Something inside me drooped when I realized that.

In the pantry, I cried until my mother opened the door, looking shocked. I glared up at her, feeling resentment for making me such an outsider even in our Korean community.

"*Yah!*" She turned to Sandy and Crystal, who stood in the kitchen, looking at the floor. "You no treat friend like this! This not nice thing!"

My mother's accent was another source of embarrassment for me. I could hear what everyone was thinking: *How has she never learned English properly the entire time she's lived here?* But of course I didn't consider the evenings my mother took my brother and me to our local community college and we sat on the floors of the classroom eating Almond Roca while she studied English. And despite my humiliation, whenever a person would raise their voice to speak to her, acting as if she were hearing-impaired, I would react with anger. Once, in an optometrist's office, the office assistant nearly screamed at my mother to file her insurance paperwork, because my mother couldn't understand what she was saying. I finally had enough. I raised my voice and yelled back at her, articulating the part of the paperwork my mother didn't understand, which had nothing to do with how well she'd heard the office assistant. I could feel the heat in my chest and my belly. But of course, as we walked away from the office, my indignance reverted back to shame because, in my eyes, my mother had embarrassed us both.

I was ashamed of my parents because they kept me from fitting into what looked "American"; it would take years before I realized that the only person I should've been ashamed of was myself.

Later that week, I was cradling my right hand in the other because it was swollen and blistered. I was sitting on the blue Circle Time rug in class, along with the rest of the fourth graders. My friend was sitting next to me on the rug and peered over into my lap.

"That looks like a waterbed. A waterbed for a fish!" my friend declared. I felt embarrassed until she grabbed my hand and started gently poking my blister with her finger. Surprisingly, it didn't hurt, and I was glad I didn't have to explain what had happened.

The day before was Halloween, and I had gotten a caramel-covered, apple-flavored lollipop. The thing was, I only wanted the caramel off the lollipop and thought it would be clever if I simply melted the caramel off rather than wait for it to melt in my mouth. I decided a microwave would be the quickest method to doing this, and after realizing I was too short to reach the plates, I looked for something to act as one. After rummaging in the drawers, I found the lid of a cream cheese container. Perfect.

I placed the lollipop on the lid and swung the microwave door shut. I punched in one minute, then hesitated. Surely, it would take longer than that to melt caramel. I pressed CLEAR and punched in five minutes instead. I watched my lollipop rotate in the microwave, giddy at my resourcefulness. But once the microwave beeped and I removed the lid by gripping the edge with one hand, the center of the lid began to droop. I had accidentally melted the entire makeshift plate along with my now liquified lollipop. I looked down at the floor beneath the lid and realized in a panic that the plastic was about to drip onto my mother's carpet. And I knew how she felt about stains.

Without thinking, I darted my hand underneath the plastic and cupped the molten-hot liquid as it dripped onto my hand. I grimaced and ran to the bathroom to run my hand under cool water, but it was too late; I had burned the flesh off my palm. But instead of tears, relief came. I smiled, as I had successfully avoided my mother's temper. I never came to find out what she thought of my injury—I tucked my hand away whenever she came near me.

My friend, who was still poking at my blister, dropped my hand as we were interrupted by my teacher's voice.

"This book," my teacher began with a flourish, "is written by Amy Tan." I lifted my head and was astonished to see an Asian face on the back of the book jacket, as the teacher expected us to ooh and aah. *A face like mine.* I was in fourth grade and had never seen an Asian person in our lessons before. I figured that none of them were famous enough because they hadn't done anything worth knowing about.

The teacher was honoring the heritage of Gary Locke, who was the newly elected governor of Seattle. He was Seattle's first Chinese American governor. It was 1997.

Later that week, my mother took Chris and me to Blockbuster Video. I rented *The Joy Luck Club*, the movie based on Amy Tan's best-selling novel by the same name. Even though the movie was not a film for fourth graders, my mother didn't monitor anything I watched. I suspected this was because she didn't know what to make of the synopsis on the back of the movie box since her English wasn't very strong.

The narratives in *The Joy Luck Club* were centered around Chinese stories, but they felt inherently mine. The feeling of being pressured to be more Asian, then less Asian. The pressure from your mother to become what she envisions you to be. The quiet suffering of being the daughter of a tiger mom. Seeing your family's Asian-ness through your white friends' eyes when you introduce your friends to your parents. The fear of bringing home a white husband. I never once thought I would be writing my own stories, because I felt as though Amy Tan had written them all for me. All her stories were my stories. And my mother's. They were the stories of my mother's generational trauma that she had passed down to me.

My mother is a woman of mystery. Her identity is shrouded in guesswork and ambivalence. She would vaguely refer to experiences in her childhood, but did I really know who my mother was? All I knew was that her past was burdened with this unknown pain. I knew this because one of the many things that we never discussed are the white scars that decorate my mother's wrists. Only years later would she confirm my suspicions, when she felt I was strong enough to handle the truth. At the time, she called her moody phases "melancholy"; I didn't realize she was using a euphemism to soften the truth's rough edges. When I was in my thirties, it dawned on me that my mother's melancholy was more commonly identified in America as depression.

TIGHTY-WHITIES

My father was wearing his tighty-whities and standing in the living room with two police officers and my frantic mother. Only moments before, I awoke in the middle of the night to a low murmur somewhere in the house. I walked down the hallway, unsure if I was dreaming. But when I saw two police officers standing in the living room towering over my parents, I knew immediately what had happened, because we'd been through this before. *I wonder what they stole this time*, I thought as I stared at the red and blue lights bouncing against our living room walls like a disco.

I quietly listened in on the conversation.

"Was there anything else that was stolen?" one officer asked, motioning around the room with his pad and pencil.

"Just VCR and TV," my mother answered tensely. "I woke up, my husband outside banging on door. Burglar push him outside."

I glanced at my father, in his tighty-whities.

"You wrestled with the burglar?" The officer raised an eyebrow at my father, who looked disappointed in himself. "Well," the officer continued, "I think the burglar snuck in through here." He began to walk down the hallway into the bathroom, and we automatically followed. He pointed to the long rectangular window above our shower stall. "I would just make sure to keep that shut at nighttime."

My father nodded. "Yes, sir. We will."

After the officers left, my mother confirmed what I suspected: the burglar wrestled with my father and locked him outside. My mother was woken up by my dad in his underwear, pounding on the door to let him into his own house.

In fact, it was strange seeing my father in the house at all. Since he worked seven days a week at two jobs, he was usually at work, or sleeping in the bedroom. And even when he was home, I would frequently forget his existence. My mother pulled so much of my focus that even my friends would assume he had passed away. I would refer to my house as my "mother's house" without even thinking twice. I never shared stories about my father because there were no stories to tell; he was always absent from our lives and our dinner table. He was a ghost.

I looked him up and down in the living room. My father was not a short man, but in that moment, he appeared small. He wanted to defend his family but instead felt as though he'd brought shame upon us by failing to apprehend the burglar. I didn't know how to tell him that this type of failure was not the one I would be embarrassed by; rather, I would be more embarrassed by the holes in his tighty-whities where the cloth gave way at the waistband. The holes that would not let me forget the type of life we lived. A reminder that there is an "us" and a "them" in the social hierarchy.

At this point in my life, being the daughter of immigrants meant being poor and living in a crap neighborhood filled with trash, crime, and spray paint. My entire identity revolved around being the poor kid. My childhood was spent being terrified that my church friends or my school friends would find out where I lived. It wouldn't be until I grew older when being a child of immigrants became much more complicated.

THE ROLLER COASTER

Later that year, in the summer I would enter fifth grade, we flew to Korea to visit my aunt and uncle. The weather was unbearably hot and humid. I stepped out of the shower there and felt immediately wet and sticky. *What was the point of a shower?* I thought dismally. I then sat in my aunt's room patiently while my mother brushed my hair. My appearance was one of the many things she liked to control. She needed to have my hair in a tight, perfect ponytail, and I had no choice in the matter.

My grandmother died from a stroke when my mother was just a teenager. Like a cigarette leaving a scorch mark on a sofa, my life would be forever tarnished by an experience I wasn't around for.

"You so lucky. You so lucky you have me. My mother die when I was nineteen." My mother would say this to me in a disapproving tone whenever she felt as though I wasn't grateful enough for everything she did for me. She used my grandmother's death as an excuse to feed her controlling behavior, and through my mother, my grandmother was far from dead; she was ever-present in our home.

By then I'd known that my mother was born in North Korea in 1953, although in 1953, the country was known as Korea; this was before dictators had taken control of the country and before a rift developed between the dictators and the people who opposed them. She had seven siblings, two brothers and five sisters, and her father was a government official while her mother raised the children at home.

Two of my mother's siblings, a brother and a sister, died from starvation. When the borders of North Korea began to close and the country withdrew into itself, my grandmother selected her two youngest children to escape with. My grandmother escaped the emergence of Communism with two daughters, leaving the other siblings behind. Her logic was that the eldest child would have a higher chance of survival in a country that was falling apart. She carried my mother, the youngest, on her back, and held the hand of her older daughter and ran away on foot. My grandfather was imprisoned and beaten for renouncing loyalty to the government that he worked for, then escaped to meet his wife and two daughters in South Korea at a later time. He died of a stroke soon after.

We would never find out if my aunts and uncle survived in North Korea since communication with the Communist country would become near impossible for civilians in the years to come.

I'd seated myself right in front of my mother as she used the comb to impatiently smooth my hair. The tugging and yanking combined with the heat of the day got to me. Impatience grew and swelled in my chest. Finally, I screamed. I yanked my hair out of the ponytail and roared again.

"Oh!" she gasped. *"Yo-goh-moh-yah!" What do you call this behavior?*

"Nah sheeruh!" I don't like this! And I dared to do the one thing that would guarantee my punishment: I looked her dead square in the eyes, something that is interpreted as a challenge in Korean culture. But I was American. She

didn't understand that I was a hybrid. She didn't understand the implications of her immigrating to America and raising a Korean American daughter. And she hated what I had become: someone who wasn't Korean enough, someone who was too Westernized in her ways.

My mother, shocked at my unacceptable behavior, grabbed the flyswatter that was leaning against the wall and shrieked while she smacked me on the thighs with the handle end.

When she would go into these blind rages, if I dared try to explain my side of things, she would accuse me of talking back and would verbally disown me, declaring me to be my father's daughter. She'd tell me I had learned to be disobedient from his awful temper, despite our home constantly being filled with her shouting. That day in Korea was no different.

I never understood why my mother was convinced my father had a bad temper, because I didn't know what "gaslighting" was back then. Gaslighting is a form of emotional abuse where an individual deflects all responsibility for their actions onto someone else. And my mother would never see the irony as she would complain about my father's anger while she screamed. She would simply expect me to take my verbal lashings and dutifully accept every insult she had hurled at me. That is what a good daughter would do. And my father, whose narrow eyes usually crinkled in joy as he spoke, the corners of his mouth curling upward, rippling into his cheeks, would endure her anger alongside me. He would stand by, his glistening bald head bowed as my mother raged on. He would wait until she left the room before whispering in my ear, "I know she is difficult. But she is a good woman."

After my lashings, I threw myself onto the bed and cried into the pillows.

"*Nah-wah-jeemah!*" *Don't you dare come out!* She slammed the door closed and left me alone with my thoughts.

I stayed in the room crying, feeling the stinging on my thighs. I could see the outline of the handle imprinted on my skin and thought about how un-American it was to beat your children and how my mother should be arrested. I noticed the room was growing darker and darker as I did not turn the light on. Sleepy from having cried so long, I drifted off.

I was woken gently by my mother.

"Cake *moh-goh sheeh-poh?*" *Do you want to get some cake?*

"*Neh,*" I sniffed. *Okay.*

Did she have amnesia? Did she not remember the flying rage she worked herself into when she saw her prim and proper daughter throw a tantrum over hair? I went along with her to the Korean bakery. I picked out a brown cake, assuming it was chocolate, but it turned out to be tiramisu. My brother complained, but my mother said she loved the taste of coffee. This was her effort to make amends, but I just felt confused because she appeared to be bipolar.

The next day, we all pretended as if nothing had happened. My brother pretended he hadn't heard my mother give me the thrashing of a lifetime. My aunt and uncle took us to an amusement park called Lotte World. The entire family was eager to go on a roller coaster, and I had never been on one. When the ride began, I immediately knew I'd made a mistake by going on it. The feeling of my stomach continually dropping and the feeling of free-falling gave me such a fright, I burst into tears. My uncle, who was sitting next to me on the ride, leaned over, screaming and laughing with delight, "*Heem-peh-rah!*" which loosely translates to *Let your strength go!*

I looked incredulously at this elderly man, laughing hard and throwing his hands into the air. He looked so . . . *free.* I did as I was told. I slowly released my grip on the seat's bars and raised my arms. I let go. I let go of the tenseness in my body, and I let go of control. I flopped around like a rag doll, and I found, miraculously, that the more I relaxed, the more secure I felt in the seat because I wasn't fighting against the force of the ride.

When the ride ended, I told my mother the advice my uncle had given me. It stuck with both of us. After that, whenever we felt as though life was getting crazy and we panicked over the sense of losing control, we would say, "*Heem-peh-rah!*"

My mother always told me the story of the willow and the wind. The willow that fights against the wind ends up breaking apart. But the willow that bends to the will of the wind is the one that survives. Bend to the wind. *Heem-peh-rah*. Because what else can you do but let go of the things you can't control?

NOT THAT KIND
OF KOREAN

F all arrived, and with that, the start of a new school year. When winter came, we had a new student whose name was Becky. And I hated her. I hated her because she outed me as a fraud. I looked up at Ms. Hertz's face, who looked at me expectantly. Ms. Hertz was my fifth-grade teacher. Becky and I stood by her desk at the front of the classroom.

"Tell her," she urged. "Tell Becky what I just said." I felt the stone at the bottom of my stomach, the tightness in my chest. "Joan, translate! You're both Korean—she needs your help because you speak English and she doesn't!"

I looked down at my feet, miserably. I shuffled my feet, my toes pointing inward, hoping the floor would open up and swallow me whole. I opened my mouth, hoping the words would come, but I was petrified, and I closed my mouth again. I looked like a frog. How could I tell her that I only spoke Korean conversationally with my mother but that I couldn't even understand when someone outside of my family spoke Korean to me? I didn't have the Korean vocabulary to be able to translate assignments. How could I tell her that I had a crippling insecurity of my ability to speak Korean, fully aware that everyone expected me to speak it perfectly, but I couldn't? *I am not that kind of Korean!* I wanted to scream. But I said nothing. Instead, I turned slowly to Becky and said something that my own ears didn't even recognize. Now she was looking at the floor.

"Good," Ms. Hertz said, satisfied that she assisted a minority student with her assimilation into American school. "You are going to be Becky's translator this year. Her family just moved here from Korea, and she's so lucky she has someone in the class who can help her." I winced as if Ms. Hertz had struck me. I glanced sideways at Becky, who was still looking at the floor. Her inability to learn English had now burdened me and brought me ceaseless embarrassment.

I hate you, I thought, glaring mutinously at Becky's expressionless face.

It would take a journey into adulthood to realize that Becky was never the true source of my deep shame at being a quasi-Korean. That came from the expectations placed on me to be something other than what my identity allowed. Being Korean is actually a spectrum of experiences and, at the same time, belonging because none of us truly conform to the expectation of what it means to be a perfect Korean. It's the fallacy that curses us all and allows for us to self-flagellate in an effort to obtain something unobtainable. And I had allowed a girl who also felt as though she had no place in this country to become the scapegoat for my insecurities.

If I ever saw Becky now, I wouldn't be surprised if she spoke perfect English and had scrubbed every remnant of an accent. I wouldn't be surprised if she harbored resentment and hated Korean girls like me who, from her perspective, had an easier time assimilating in a country that is known to crucify any hint of otherness. If I were Becky, I would hate me too.

KOREAN SCHOOL

few years later, I was leaning back in my chair in Korean school. I was ten years old, and the boy behind me was batting my ponytail like a cat. He was slightly overweight but short and had fringe bangs. Without thinking, I abruptly turned in my chair and slapped him across the face with all my strength. A couple of Korean teachers rushed over to see if he was okay. Then came the scolding and tutting at me, and the fretting over the boy, who was dissolving into tears. I just stood over him, not feeling an ounce of sorry. Little did I know, that boy would later become my best friend at Korean school.

Korean school was a chore. It was a rite of passage if you were Korean and in grade school in America. It meant that, in addition to going to school Monday through Friday like everyone else, you had to go to school on Saturday as well. Classes were held at a local high school, and all the Korean children in the area from all different elementary schools pooled into the building. All of us sacrificed our Saturdays, studying the Korean language, culture, and, specifically, tae kwon do—the point being to drill into us our Korean heritage.

The teachers were strict, smacking yardsticks on their desks to punctuate their lessons, standing in front of rows and rows of austere ponytails and attentive eyes.

"*Ahnyung-hah-seh-yoh!*" they would call out every morning.

"*Ahnyung-hah-seh-yoh!*" we would call back in unison.

All the children would recite Korean obediently, sitting erect in their seats like perfect little dolls. I was usually found slumped in my chair next to Roy, the boy I had slapped. Roy got over my slap when I had convinced him that he deserved it, and then we started spending class time passing notes, whispering jokes, and shouting the answers to the teacher's questions out of turn. The other boys and girls glared at us for being rowdy and disruptive. We lacked self-control, which is highly valued at Korean school.

"*Nah deung-koh gahree-whoa,*" he said under his breath to me. *My butthole is itchy.* I burst out laughing. The Korean school teacher shot daggers at me with her eyes. I hiccupped a laugh and pretended to look ahead at the chalkboard. She sighed. It was time for announcements, and she told us that the Korean school talent show was coming up and teachers were asking kids to try out so they could preview their routines, but that every child would get to participate. I shoved an elbow in Roy's rib cage and raised my eyebrows, nodding in the direction of the teacher. He nodded his head eagerly in agreement, then didn't miss a beat to pull a face, pursing his lips, crossing his eyes, and waving his hand at me. I struggled not to laugh. The boys and girls around us turned in their chairs and tsked at us. I stuck my tongue out at them. This was it. This would be the perfect way for us to show our school that we were special and that the other students and teachers had disregarded our gifts.

The following Monday, at American school, I was in the cafeteria getting ready to sit down to eat lunch when I noticed two tall girls standing over Roy while he was crying.

They were standing outside the cafeteria doors. I dropped my lunch tray down on a nearby table and stomped outside.

"What are you doing?" I demanded, looking at the two girls and then at Roy. One was blonde, the other was a brunette, and both looked guilty.

"It's nothing," he sniffed.

"We just want him to be honest," the brunette shot back defensively.

"About what?" I asked.

"About being gay," the blonde responded, almost tentatively. "He's lying to us."

"Who cares?" I spat. "And it's none of your business. And he's not gay, and you're bullying him! Get away from him! Now!" The girls muttered something and dispersed.

"Are you okay?" I asked Roy gently.

"Yeah," he almost whispered. We walked back into the cafeteria, and I pushed the altercation to the back of my mind.

In the following weeks, Roy and I spent every day after school practicing and rehearsing for the Korean school talent show. We decided to choreograph a dance that was a mix of the moves we saw on *Buffy the Vampire Slayer* and our two dancing styles. This would be a way for us to finally express ourselves at Korean school after months of feeling like we were the random sweet potato fries scattered in your order that you never wanted.

The day finally arrived after one month of practice. We were standing on the outskirts of the gymnasium. Girls and boys showcased their boring talents by singing Korean folk songs, playing piano, dancing traditional Korean fan dances, and playing some flutes here and there. But finally it was our turn. Roy and I held hands, walked front and center of the

Korean teachers, and smiled. We looked at each other and took a deep breath.

The band 98 Degrees' "True to Your Heart" began on the stereo. Roy and I faced each other and gyrated to the music, locking hands, then pushing away to spin. He kicked his leg over my head as I ducked. We didn't see any faces; we just focused on pelvic thrusting in sync. For one spectacular moment, we were rainbow-colored, and everyone else watching was beige. When the music finally came to a stop, we were breathing hard and holding our *Buffy* poses like the women of *Charlie's Angels*. The faces of the Korean teachers were blank, and the room was silent.

"Thank you!" I shouted graciously into the dead quiet, waving as we walked off the gymnasium floor.

The next day, my mother broke the news to me. The teachers didn't want Roy and me performing in the talent show. At all.

"But the song was from *Mulan!*" I exclaimed. That year was my last year at Korean school. Roy told me later that it would be his last year as well. We weren't too bothered because we never felt like we belonged there anyway. It wasn't until high school that Roy would come out as gay, and it was then when I understood why we gravitated toward each other at Korean school.

Neither of us fit into the mold of the ideal Korean child. In our misfit-ness, we had found each other. Being the ideal Korean child meant getting good grades to make good on our parents' sacrifice when they immigrated to this country to provide their children with a chance at the coveted American education. It meant showing filial piety, or respect for your parents, which manifests into eternal indebtedness for their sacrifice. It meant marrying a good Christian Korean—of the opposite sex. In Korean Evangelism's heteronormativity, we were supposed to fulfill our parents' expectations of providing grandchildren (despite the fact that gay people can also have babies).

For me, being the ideal Korean child meant fulfilling my father's dreams that he never achieved. He wanted a doctorate. He wanted to be in upper-level management. Instead, he looked to me. But he never once asked that I achieve those things. Neither did my mother. I just knew the crushing burden not to waste their sacrifice—the burden that was all the more suffocating because I already knew I was far from my parents' expectations of me.

NIPPLES AND TAMPONS

My mother decided that her daughter must escape the lowly neighborhood public school system, so she used what little English she had to figure out the transfer system to put me into a wealthier school district. When I finally got to middle school, I was relieved to find that my school had a large Asian population. Almost 50 percent of our student demographic was Asian. But when I found out that all my Asian friends were rich, just as was the case at church, I quickly reverted to feeling bitter and displaced.

In seventh grade, I took shop class as an elective. I quickly befriended two of my classmates, Brie and Tyson. Brie had a toothy grin and long, curly blonde hair. Tyson was so pale he looked like he might not have a pulse. He also had blue hair and soulful brown eyes. Brie and Tyson were girlfriend and boyfriend, which amazed me since my mother would never approve of me dating. During our shop periods, Brie and Tyson would regale me with stories of their sexual encounters. Brie would tell me how amazing fingering was. It was a miracle I never accidentally sawed anything off in that class.

One day, Brie looked at me sympathetically and leaned over.

"Joan, I hate to tell you this, but do you know that the guys all call you Nippy?"

"What? Why?" I asked, confused.

"Um . . . because . . . your nipples are always showing? Girl, you are not wearing the right bras." And there it was again, the hot shame of being a freak. Until that moment, I had no idea that wearing a thin sweater and the wrong bra was not a good combination for a cold classroom. I groaned.

"What kind of bra do you wear?" I asked her. And in the middle of class, she pulled down her shirt to show me a lacy, sexy bra. My eyes grew big.

"It's padded," she explained. "So, even if it is cold, my nipples won't show." I grew angry. Why didn't my mother talk to me about this? If she was going to insist on choosing my bras and my clothes for school, why wouldn't she buy the correct bra for me? I felt as though I didn't have a proper mother to help me navigate the hazards of having breasts.

Thanks a lot, Umma, I thought gloomily.

Later that year, summer was approaching and the weather was warming up. This meant that our class field trip to Wild Waves, a water amusement park, was imminent. I sat in social studies with my friend Brian, and he was telling me how he tried to masturbate with a bottle of Gold Bond but ended up burning himself badly.

"That's great, Brian," I said sarcastically. "Really. Really, great. Thanks for that." Then it hit me. That familiar, gentle gush in my underwear. Quickly, I grabbed the hall pass and ran to the girls' bathroom. *No . . . no . . . it can't be, not yet!* Our field trip to the water park was that week—and how was I supposed to go swimming wearing a maxi pad? Once, I had tried to convince my mother to let me switch to tampons, but she forbade it. She thought tampons were disgusting, and I knew with certainty she felt that way because she feared my using them would mean I wasn't a virgin anymore. But I knew this time I had to take matters into my own hands.

I managed to obtain a single tampon from a friend before the field trip and hid it in my pocket, where my mother wouldn't find it. Right before we loaded up the buses on the day of the excursion, I excused myself to go into the bathroom. But when I got there, I had no idea what to do. I looked curiously at the tampon (which did not come with an applicator) and studied it carefully. Because I didn't have the box it came in, which would have had step-by-step directions, I had to guess how it worked. *I suppose . . . this way?* Instead of actually inserting the tampon straight into the vaginal opening, I carefully wedged the tampon sideways between my two vaginal lips, with the string hanging out the back. My friend, whom I got the tampon from, swore by tampons, saying you couldn't even feel anything when you wore them, but I would care to disagree. I felt like I had a mousetrap in my underwear, pinching me mercilessly. I shrugged the feeling off and headed toward the buses.

When we arrived at Wild Waves, we all split into groups. My friends and I rode roller coasters, but all the while I was squirming uncomfortably with the foreign object in my bathing suit bottoms fighting against me. I did my best to ignore the tampon, which I finally did successfully when we arrived at the wave pool. I walked carefully into the water, about waist-deep. I watched how everyone was laughing and jumping when a wave would catch up to them, so I tried jumping as well. But when I jumped, the wave caught me and pulled me under. I struggled for a second to plant my feet back on the ground, and when I stood up out of the water, I was coughing and sputtering. I immediately realized something was wrong. My tampon was no longer in my bathing suit. I froze. Did I dare look around? Did I dare try to grab it before someone else noticed? But what if someone noticed me searching? Wouldn't they know the tampon belonged to me?

To avoid the *Caddyshack* moment when everyone would begin screaming at the floater in the pool, I scrambled out of the wave pool. I caught my friend by the elbow on the way out.

"I'm not in the mood for this anymore. Come with me to get some cotton candy!"

"Erm, okay!" she agreed. I walked away with my friend and tried not to look back.

Internally, I shook my head. Mishaps in puberty could only be placed at my mother's door. Why wasn't she better prepared to raise a daughter? I would only wonder for a few moments before remembering that my grandmother died when my mother was nineteen years old . . . but wait, that would mean that my grandmother *was* alive for my mother's adolescence. So why did she know so little about raising a teenage daughter?

Then my pace slowed down. My friend looked at me curiously as an incredible sadness took grip over me.

My mother's youth was poverty and escaping North Korea. My youth was the Nokia brick phone and begging for a car when I turned sixteen. My mother's youth was her siblings dying from disease. My youth was the iPod Shuffle and going to Sam Goody for the new Backstreet

Boys CD. My mother's youth was her father in a government prison.

My mother didn't have a chance to have an adolescence. My mother was twenty when she was twelve.

"What's wrong?" my friend asked.

"Nothing," I said quietly.

ARIZONA

Middle school was over before I had time to find a white boyfriend and have a full teenage rebellion against my mother. Although, during one spectacular fight with my mother, my father awoke from his slumber and walked into my room and yelled, "This is why you fighting with your mother!" as he waved his hand over my NSYNC poster. I was slack-jawed and wondered if he had ever heard of Marilyn Manson.

I was a freshman in high school when I was sitting in my room struggling to do my homework. The silence in our house was interrupted by the ringing of the phone. I looked at my watch. It was ten o'clock at night, and my father was long asleep in my parents' bedroom. *Who could be calling at this hour?* I wondered. I could hear my mother pick up the landline in the other room.

"He not home," she said abruptly. She sounded irritated. And with that, she slammed the phone down, and silence fell upon the house once more like a heavy blanket.

I cracked open the window of my bedroom. My father had worked steadily over the years so our family became financially secure. With the additional income, my parents decided to renovate and add on several hundred more feet to our home—two bedrooms and an additional bathroom. I finally had my own room instead of sharing a room with my parents (growing up, it was the norm that my mother allowed my brother to have his own bedroom, since she believed he deserved privacy). Rain was pouring down heavily, and I sat at the edge of my bed, romanticizing the sound. At night, I could frequently hear a distant train whistle, calling out its loneliness. That sound, paired with the rain, stirred within me a happy sadness. The phone rang again, and my feelings turned sour.

"Chris?" my mother asked, uncertainly. Then the rushed stream of frantic Korean. Immediately, I sensed something was wrong. I looked over at the phone in my room, tempted to listen in on the conversation to piece together what was unfolding. I knew that if I didn't get answers then, that night would go down in our family history as another secret we never talk about. I made a decision.

I crept over to my nightstand and gingerly lifted the receiver to my ear. My mother was speaking in Korean, and my brother was speaking in English, but I could barely understand the words he was saying. "Counterfeit . . . drugs . . . a deal . . ." My big brother, my infallible brother, was hysterically crying on the other end of the line.

"Come home," my mother said sternly. She was using that tone—what she'd said was no longer debatable. He automatically agreed. Then he hung up.

I burst from my room and demanded to know. "Umma! What is going on?" And there it was, the silence that cursed my family. The conversation, I could see, would be stored away in her mental lockbox, where I would never be able to retrieve it.

"If anyone ask, Chris move to Mexico."

"What?" I exclaimed. "Are you insane? This is crazy! Umma, what is happening?" She didn't respond. I eventually gave up, and we both settled on the couch and waited, jittery, sitting in silence. I began to bounce my knees in impatience, as I always do.

"Joan! *Gohmanheh!*" She smacked my thighs. I stopped. It was seconds later before I started up again, but I was stopped when our phone's ring tore through the silence once more. I darted a glance over to the phone, only partially understanding what was happening. My mother walked over calmly and picked up the phone.

"Chris in Mexico," she said, then she placed the phone back in the cradle.

What seemed like hours later, the garage door rumbled to life. My mother and I quickly strode to the door to greet him. Chris, soaked from the rain, breathing heavily, didn't even stop to look at me. He rushed past me into his room. I hung back, uncertain, not knowing what to say or whether or not I had a right to know what was going on. I stood in the living room, seeing into his bedroom as he threw a suitcase on his bed and began to pack his things. My mother was whispering again in that frantic Korean. I felt as though I were an outsider, looking into a family I didn't know. My head felt as though it were submerged in water, and I was not hearing things clearly.

The next thing I knew, we were standing in the garage, in the cold. I watched as the headlights of my brother's car pulled away from the driveway, the coloring of the lights peppered by the rain. *Of course*, I thought wryly. *Of course on a night like tonight it would rain.*

"He going to Arizona, Joan. To be with cousin Brandon." My mother didn't even look at me, just out into the rain as the garage door closed. I said nothing in response.

I walked back into the house with my mother. We walked our separate ways into our bedrooms and closed the doors. I realized my window was still open, and water was pooling on the edge of the windowsill. I stood in front of the window, feeling numb. I then heard the lonely train's whistle call out to me as though it understood what I was feeling.

The next day in school, I was exhausted from the lack of sleep. As I walked through the school commons, a friend of mine ran up to me.

"Did you hear?" she asked eagerly. I froze. Headlines of a criminal being caught on a drive to Arizona flashed through my mind.

"No . . ." I said slowly.

"Two planes crashed into the Twin Towers!" she blurted out, almost gleeful, it seemed, to be the one to break the news to me. I instantly felt relief.

All over the country, people were devastated by the news of the thousands of people who would die that day in the terrorist attacks on 9/11, and all I could feel was relief.

That fall, in 2001, my mother told me we were visiting my brother and my mother's nephew, Brandon, in Arizona. She said that *Appa*, my father, would stay home and continue to go to work. We had not been on a plane together since our trip to Korea. I felt nervous because I didn't know what to expect. Were we going to talk about that night Chris drove out of our lives? Was I going to get answers? We had spent months spreading the lie about my brother moving to Mexico to friends and family members until people stopped asking how my brother was doing. My mother and I never spoke about that night, and I never even thought to ask.

The plane ride was a blur. It was automatic, robotic even. It wasn't until the drive to Brandon's house that I could feel the weight of my breaths in my chest. I stared out the window as the landscape rushed by. Where we lived in Washington, everything was a rich green, the mountains decorating the backdrop. Here, everything looked dead. And brown. The landscape was flat and lifeless. It was as if I had taken a pencil and dragged it across the sky out of the window of the car as it was driving by. "So, this is where Chris lives now," I murmured, completely unimpressed.

"We're here! Chris at work. He meet us later," my mother said excitedly. *Here we go,* I thought, and took a deep breath.

When we pulled up to the driveway, I felt sick to my stomach. I had no idea what to expect, and we were staying in my cousin's house, a cousin I hadn't seen in about a decade. When we stepped out of the car and walked toward the house, a man opened the door.

"Brandon!" my mother cried out. I stopped dead in my tracks when my eyes fell on Brandon. I was stunned. I suddenly recalled the time I'd seen Brandon's face for the first time, all those Christmases ago. His face had hovered over me as I sat on the floor. It was almost Christmas, and I was five years old. I was huddled in front of the heater because our house was always freezing in the wintertime since we lived in a cinder block house.

"Go on, take it," he'd said gently. He had a kind voice. He reached out, handing me a festively wrapped gift, and I felt bashful. *What is this man doing in our house in the dead of winter?* I'd thought. We never had guests. My mother was always embarrassed to show people where we lived, since we couldn't afford a fancy house with stairs and we lacked basic furniture. Our entire house barely fit our family of four.

"This your cousin Brandon," my mother had said. "Say thank you!"

I slowly looked up and mustered a meek "Thank you," and my eyes roamed around his face. He was different. He looked different. But I couldn't quite put my finger on why. That day in Arizona, I saw what that "different" was. Standing in the driveway, ten years later, I realized: Brandon was a Black man. I dropped my backpack on the ground. My mother burst out laughing at my reaction. "You didn't know Brandon Black? He half-Korean! Look at his eyes!" How did she know what I was thinking? *We had Black family members this entire time?*

"Oh . . ." I couldn't find anything else to follow up with as I unabashedly stared at his face. How was our mixed family never mentioned? Brandon was dying laughing at me, clutching his stomach, as if he had been a part of some prank.

"Come on in," he said, as he put an arm around my shoulder and ushered me into the house. As we walked down the hallway past the foyer, a beautiful Black woman stood in a doorway with a bright, colorful wrap over her hair.

Brandon introduced her. "This is my wife." She smiled at me and shook my hand. Then two little figures pushed past us, giggling and shouting. "Those are my babies!" Brandon raised his voice over the noise. I couldn't believe it. If Brandon was half-Asian and he was my mother's nephew, that would mean my mother's sister, a Korean woman, married a Black man. How did I never hear the story of the interracial marriage that occurred when interracial marriage had just become legalized in a country that only just got rid of segregation? But at the same time, the fact that I didn't know the story didn't entirely surprise me, because I belong to a family that never speaks.

Suddenly, a small *ahjoomah*, or Korean elderly woman, stepped into the living room. My mother immediately gasped, throwing her hands over her mouth, then let out a wail that sounded like a wounded animal. That wail would be forever ingrained in my memory. In that moment, I heard the pain, suffering, and resilience in a note that transmitted the weight of the past and present carried by two sisters. In that wail, I heard my grandmother's sacrifice when she escaped North Korea.

I stood with my cousin and his family in the living room, surrounding my mother and her sister as they embraced each other, falling into each other's arms, weeping. Heaving. These were the two who escaped. The woman hugging my mother was Brandon's mother.

The uncanny likeness between the two women startled me. My aunt's face looked as if someone had held a mirror up to my mother. And in that moment, I realized she was the one my mother would discreetly call and ask for money when I had holes in my shoes, when I'd come home from school with my socks soaking wet. I'd pretended I didn't overhear those phone calls, but I knew. My aunt had been living in Arizona all this time, and my mother never told me anything about her except for their escape from North Korea.

Later that night, we sat around the dining room table. My brother finally returned from work, much to my mother's delight. I avoided talking to him about what we were doing in Arizona in the first place, so instead I stuck to small talk. He seemed relieved. In the absence of information, I chose to mentally fill in the gaps myself based on what I overheard on the phone that night he left. The only logical explanation that I could think of was that he'd been involved in a drug deal that had gone bad after accidentally exchanging drugs for counterfeit money. And I never found out otherwise.

When yawns began interrupting the conversation, we all agreed it was time for bed. But while the rest of the family turned in, Brandon and I stayed in the living room. He was sitting on the couch, and I was standing in front of the credenza, marveling at the family photographs. My family's photographs. As my eyes drifted over the picture frames, one caught my attention: my mother's sister and her Black husband. My aunt was sitting in the forefront, and Brandon's father was standing behind her, one hand on her shoulder. The photograph was aged and tinged with a cream-colored haze. As if Brandon could read my mind, he stood up and walked over to me.

"They married in the seventies. When they'd walk down the street, strangers would spit in their faces," he explained bitterly. I imagined he had told this story a thousand times before. "They loved each other so much, but it wasn't a good marriage . . ." He shook his head. "That was the day he gave her a black eye. She's wearing makeup in that photo. Can you imagine? Getting a black eye and then deciding to go get a family portrait done?" He laughed an empty laugh. The thought that his parents had fought hard to hold on to something that wasn't working and that society was fighting hard against . . . *What was the point? Why not give up?* I was struggling to understand, so I was left feeling confused. Not knowing what to say, I said nothing at all.

"My dad was a drunk," he continued. "He was tough too. I remember one time in elementary school, the kids were making fun of my eyes and doing this—" Brandon reached up and pulled the corners of his eyes outward with his fingers, making his eyes narrow. I hated that gesture so much. "I punched one of them in the face. And then I ran. I ran all the way home, ran into my house, and my dad was sitting on the couch. I told him what happened, and he said, 'Go on, take me outside,' so I led him out front where the boys had caught up to me. Then he slammed the door shut behind me." Brandon roared with laughter. "He always believed that you should solve your own problems."

I lay in bed that night, staring at the ceiling and thinking about the events of the day. The next day, we were going to Brandon's dad's grave to pay our respects. I didn't know how I felt about paying respects to a man who abused his wife, but it seemed that everyone felt it fitting we go, including my aunt. I just couldn't understand it, and maybe it was okay that I didn't.

Early the next morning, we drove out to the cemetery. We walked through the field of headstones, wilted flowers, and forgotten teddy bears. I didn't know what we were looking for. But when we arrived, I knew. The group eventually came to a stop, and there was a brief pause of silence.

Suddenly, my aunt dropped to her knees and threw herself onto my uncle's grave and sobbed as if her chest were being cracked open. All of her emotions were flooding out onto the grave, as if she were telling him exactly how she felt about their life together, the way she was treated, even his death. Her shoulders shook as we stood over her, watchful and mournful, and suddenly, I understood. I looked at my aunt and then I looked at my mother, realizing sadly that you can't control who you love.

When my aunt's sobs quieted, she sat up and wiped her face, still sitting in the grass. She then pulled a pack of cigarettes out of her purse. She slowly slid out a single cigarette and lit it dramatically, tilting her head to the sky. She took a long drag, then nestled it in the grass, in front of the headstone. "There," she said, matter-of-factly. "Now we can smoke together again."

ASIANS ARE GOOD AT MATH

My trip to Arizona affected me profoundly, but soon it was neatly wrapped and nestled deep in my memories; there was so much to unpack, but I didn't know what to make of it, so I tucked it away for safekeeping.

And although my brother should have been the black sheep of the family after dropping out of community college to drive to Arizona, I became the black sheep instead. I was a sophomore in high school, and I was struggling in my classes. Although my grades were decent, I noticed I had to work much harder to get the same grades as my peers. During one particularly stressful study session in which we had to memorize the Gettysburg Address, I gave up and wrote Lincoln's entire speech on my thigh and wore a denim skirt to school the next day. During the test, I continuously pulled my skirt almost up to my underwear, scribbling on my test and looking extremely interested in my crotch.

One day in class, I'd had enough. Like a sweater that slides onto the floor when you throw it on a chair, I hunkered behind my desk before descending to the linoleum. When I arrived, I lay there, my eyes squinting at the harsh fluorescent lights. I hugged my knees and pulled my hoodie over my head, ignoring the giggling I heard around the classroom.

My teacher pretended not to see me on the floor in the fetal position.

I opened one eye and peered up at my girlfriend, who was taking photos of me on her silver flip phone and sniggering. I pulled my hoodie further over my face and closed my eyes again, trying to fall asleep. I was failing AP statistics.

Just the week before, I demanded my friend Peyton give me his homework to copy. This had become my default over the past year. And I would only see the irony of this moment years later: the Asian girl copying her white friend's math homework, not the other way around, as society would believe.

"You'll never make it in college!" Peyton would hiss at me, shaking his head in utter disapproval.

"Whatever," I would mutter, without even looking up as I scrambled to jot down his answers on a sheet of notebook paper.

But I didn't ask Peyton for his homework that day in class. No . . . that day, I felt total surrender. That day, I decided I was tired of pretending I was something I was not. That day, I realized that even though every single one of my Asian friends had signed up for AP statistics, I should have known the class was a mistake for me. I couldn't do math. I recalled my mother berating me and shouting at me at the public library once when she'd tried to teach me division in third grade. I shut down and froze whenever she looked at me expectantly for the answer. The same anxiety had since riddled me in high school whenever a teacher would call on me. My mind would go blank, and I would panic. It didn't matter what the question was—it could've been "What is 2 times 350?" I wouldn't be able to answer. All the while, I was aware of what people were thinking when they looked at me. But I wasn't that kind of Asian.

How would I tell my parents that I was failing math? In fourth grade, I failed a math test. I rummaged in our kitchen drawers for a lighter, then burned the test in the bathtub. I quickly turned the faucet on, making sure all the embers were put out. Then I carefully collected the charred pieces that wouldn't fit down the drain and hid them in my pink Polly Pocket. That was what I'd done when I failed a test, but this was an entire course in high school that I wouldn't get credit for.

The bell rang, and we all herded out of the classroom. I pushed myself off the floor and followed my girlfriend. All the students rushed toward the door, and we came to a halt as the crowd narrowed to funnel out of the doorway. *Cattle. We're all cattle*, I thought.

As my friend and I walked down the main hall, the chatter was deafening. We strolled past the red-and-gold-painted walls and the mural that demanded excellence in all we did. In the middle of the hallway wing, there was a bench where our friends were already waiting.

"Guys," my girlfriend started, opening her flip phone to pull up the photograph she'd taken in class of me lying on the floor. "Look what Joan did in AP stats today. Hilarious." Our friends gathered around, snickering at my bold rebellion against authority and rules. I converted my expression from insecurity to smugness.

"Yeah." I shrugged. "I just don't give a shit." They laughed.

As far as I was concerned, at least I wasn't at the bottom of the social hierarchy at my high school. Because our high school's student demographic was similar to my middle school (50 percent Asian American), it was surprising that there was a hierarchy among the Asian Americans. The bottom of the hierarchy were students we called the FOBs. Fresh Off the Boat kids were students who had just immigrated to America. There was a disconnect between those of us who were American-born and them. FOBs were in English as a Second Language classes and were struggling to assimilate. We American-born kids were simply relieved not to be (for once) the total outsiders in a community that none of us entirely belonged to. Little did the rest of us know that the FOBs had more of an understanding of what it meant to be Asian American than we did. They intimately knew about their country's history and customs; we American-born kids were only taught the Chinese dynasties in school. And if our parents taught us nothing, then we were left in the dark, trying to figure out what it meant to be Asian American on our own. But even then, we just wanted to belong, to blend in with American culture—white culture. But being American-born still didn't earn us complete privilege among the white students.

One day, during Spanish class, I was sitting next to a white classmate of mine named Horowitz. He overheard me call myself "whitewashed" to a friend of mine. This term was used frequently among the Asian community to describe a total loss of our Asian identity and culture as we assimilated in America. Generally, those of us who used this term as an identifier had immigrant parents. Horowitz reared and lashed out at me.

"Whitewashed? How dare you! How can you use that word? Do you know what Hitler did to the Jews? You're just as bad as fucking Hitler!" he yelled.

This reaction puzzled me for years afterward. It wasn't until I used the term "whitewashed" again, only to offend another white person, that I realized what was happening. Both Horowitz and the other person took my using the term as a personal affront, and the reason they were offended was because neither of them understood the offensive part of whitewashing. What's offensive about whitewashing is that it occurs when a person of color is pressured to assimilate to white culture and does so successfully at the cost of their parents' culture. And it would be the second incident in which I offended a white person with the term "whitewashing" when I would realize that neither of them understood what ethnocentrism does to people of color.

The other interesting element: Horowitz was Jewish. When he heard me say "whitewashing," he was triggered because of what Hitler did to his people, and he associated the term with eugenics. In that moment, when he yelled at me in class, he saw me as a white supremacist in the sense of an anti-Semite. He had forgotten that I was a person of color. This is similar to how many white people forget when Asians are involved in a conversation, and they categorize us as white only when it is convenient for them. According to society, we're not quite white, but we're not quite people of color. Many white people reserve the term "people of color" for Blacks, Hispanics, and Indigenous Americans, leaving us Asian Americans, once again, neither here nor there.

THE PARTY

lthough I used to strive to be the perfect Korean, I gave up the facade my junior year in high school. What was the point in trying to be something I was clearly not?

On the night of the party, I was gliding through a dark house that almost looked like a cabin, with oppressive wood paneling and dark lighting. The carpet was heavily stained with dark liquid, and the kitchen looked as though it was from the seventies. The house was bare of any decor and was void of any personality. But it was, on that weekend, brimming with teenage life and vibrating hormones.

This was the big party house that every high school has, a house so decimated that no parent would suspect a party was there the night before. And I would venture to guess the parents wouldn't have cared even if they knew. Absent parents, naturally, were key to a high school party house.

I floated through the party, a blissful smile on my face. I felt . . . *free*. I had never tried alcohol before because I was determined to be the obedient Korean girl my mother wanted me to be. But that night . . . that night I decided I would throw that all out the window. If I was going to be constantly punished for being disobedient, why shouldn't I just embrace being bad?

My phone buzzed, and I looked down at it. Thirty-three missed calls. And my mother was calling again. She was calling me repeatedly because it was an hour past curfew. And that was what she would do, weekend after weekend— psychotically hang up and redial over and over again for hours on end. But that night, I was carefree. I held down the power button and turned my phone off. Problem solved. I was having the time of my life. I threw my hands up as "Hotel California" blasted on the stereo. People in the living room were waving to and fro. The air was hazy, polluted with billows of skunky smoke. I didn't even think twice about the couple in the corner making out, hands exploring under shirts and pants. I continued through the house, gliding through the kitchen. Dozens and dozens of bottles of booze littered the kitchen counter—Monarch vodka, peppermint schnapps, Malibu rum, just to name a few. Cans of Pabst Blue Ribbon stood forgotten. I laughed at nothing. I was free. I reached over for a bottle of rum and tilted the bottle into my mouth. I held my mouth open and poured until my mouth was full. I swallowed in one big gulp. It burned, and I felt alive. Nothing could stop me. This would become one of many weekends I would spend completely obliterated out of my mind. I couldn't escape my mother, and college couldn't come fast enough. Alcohol was the only key to complete liberation from my mother's ever-tightening grip on me, and I just wanted to pull away and figure out who I was—be the real, uninhibited me.

I was standing in the kitchen until I wasn't. I opened my eyes, as if I had blinked for an extraordinarily long period of time. Then I was walking, descending a dark hallway, down stairs. And someone was helping me walk, my arm draped around their shoulders. Everything went black again.

When I opened my eyes, I was staring at the wood-paneled ceiling in the dark. Something was inside me. Someone. Someone was looming over me.

"Do you have a condom?" I slurred, panicked. I was a virgin, but I knew about unprotected sex. The last thing I needed was to get pregnant. My mother would kill me. "Oh! I'll go get one!" The guy who was over me perked up, and it wasn't until he moved toward the door that I realized he was a school friend of mine. He hurried out of the room, leaving me on the bed. *No, that's not what I meant . . .* But I couldn't speak. I tried to get myself off the bed, but I fell face-first onto the floor, tangled in the bedsheets.

"Wait . . ." I tried to call out, but my head was foggy. I was completely wasted. I crawled to the door. I fumbled with the doorknob and pushed. I fell, stumbling out of the room. I held my hands up to shield my eyes from the bright lights.

"Oh . . . my . . . *God.*" One of the most popular girls in the grade above me was standing there, holding a beer, her mouth gaping open. I hadn't realized until that moment that I was completely naked. She rolled her eyes, looking disgusted, and ran over to another group of kids I recognized but didn't know and whispered to them. They all stared at me, pointing. Horrified, I made my way back to the room, and before I even reached for the doorknob, I blacked out again.

The pain jerked me to consciousness. I was staring at that wood-paneled ceiling again. I was in the dark again. This time the guy was grunting and moaning on top of me. And before I could even process what was happening, it was over.

That following Monday, everyone whispered about me as I walked through the halls at school. The guy who'd been in the room with me ended up transferring to a different school, and I never saw him again. Rumors about me swirled. They stung at first, but I just pretended not to hear them. I couldn't get mad. It wasn't rape. I didn't exactly say no. *But you didn't exactly say yes either*, a small voice in my head said. I ignored it. It didn't matter anyway. I wasn't an alcoholic, because I only drank on weekends, so it was okay. I continued to drink myself into a stupor when I could because the high cost of getting wasted was worth the feeling of complete freedom from my repression. What I didn't realize was a lack of a no that night did not imply consent, but my realization was too late; my mind had wrapped a protective layer around the memory of my assault to protect my body, like a cyst.

I never told my mother what had happened to me either. I assumed she—the woman who once crinkled her nose and said "yech!" when I said the word "sex" in front of her—would look at the entire situation as shameful and disgusting. I didn't allow myself to unpack my assault until decades later, when the Me Too movement ripped the lid off of assault cases similar to mine and educated the world that the gray space when you are too drunk to consent is still rape. Years later, when I would refer to my experience as "date rape," my friends who used to joke about the party where I lost my virginity would gape when it dawned on them what really happened to me that night.

FURIOUS TO DIE

Weeks passed after the party. And in an effort to forget what happened, I went to every single consecutive party afterward and drank until I blacked out.

One night, I sat at my desk, squinting as I tried to focus on my computer screen. The skin on my fingers was so dehydrated it felt like paper as I gently tapped the keyboard. I had the shakes from withdrawal, and my stomach was irritated. I ran the tip of my tongue over my cracking lips, thinking about what to type.

I stared at the Western Washington University application home page and sighed. I was only applying to two colleges because those were the only application fees we could afford. With college looming from my high school senior year, I had to fulfill my obligation to my immigrant parents to achieve the American education they had come to this country for. I had gently suggested a gap year in Europe, but my mother wouldn't hear of it.

I read the college application essay prompt out loud: "A moment that profoundly changed me . . ." But nothing came to mind. Too many years had passed since my trip to Arizona, and I had truly never given our trip a second thought since we returned. My mixed family had faded into the background just like the edges of the family portraits on the credenza in my cousin's living room. They ceased to exist, because our family was expected not to discuss what we didn't understand. So, much like my immigrant parents, I made a subconscious choice not to talk about it, not to think about it. And my assault had already been completely forgotten. It no longer existed in the realm of my mind.

I thought back to what I was doing before I sat down to write my college essay. I was sitting on the floor in front of the television and watching the news. The reporter had just explained that Lisa Ling had gone undercover into North Korea, pretending to work for a humanitarian program in order to gain access into the authoritarian government. It was 2006. I felt a twinge of jealousy as I wondered, *What about us? The ones who want to know if our family is still alive?*

Did that moment affect me profoundly, though? I wondered at my computer. Could anything affect me profoundly anymore? That's the thing about going numb and retreating into yourself so far—you might turn inside out. Because you feel so misunderstood, so alone, it becomes difficult to feel anything other than rage and resentment. And you only find comfort in chaos and all things bitter.

Later on, in my adult years, I would read Cathy Park Hong's *Minor Feelings*, and she would describe her quintessential Korean friend who had such fury to live and the same intensity to die. I felt this same fire inside. But it was burning me up alive. I knew from a young age that I wouldn't make it into my thirties. I felt resolve in this; almost as if on a subconscious level, I knew that what I had already experienced at seventeen was too heavy a burden to carry through a lifetime.

What moment had a profound impact on me? I asked myself again. Then I sat up as I remembered something from the other night. I closed my eyes as I recalled the details. And I saw the night play out behind my eyelids like a movie.

It was late and I was driving home. Not unusual, because I did everything I could to stay out of the house as much as possible to avoid my mother.

The streetlights had halos around them. It wasn't raining, a rare night in Seattle, but it was still frigid, and the cold humidity settled in your bones like a wet blanket.

As I drove down the straightaway near my family's home, something caught my eye. There was a guy in his early twenties walking and cradling a large bouquet of white lilies. The moment I saw him, he walked underneath a streetlight, and the lilies gave a heavenly glow. They still had their plastic wrap, still looked fresh. It was about two in the morning, and he was headed in the direction of the cemetery. Why did it occur to him to visit at this time of night? But then again, is there ever a right time?

Is there a right time to say sorry?

Is there a right time to say you love someone?

Did he miss his chance?

My thoughts plummeted into what could've been. He looked young. He looked regretful. He reminded me of . . . me. But the version of me that hadn't become yet—if that makes any sense.

But what came next on my college application essay is where the lie began.

"Don't take people for granted," I typed. "We spend so much time in youth assuming we are immortal. But life is a fragile thing. It is the one thing that is not guaranteed. Knowing this, how should we live our lives? I choose to live my life without regret. But yet humbled because I know my time is temporary. I want to squeeze every last drop out of life and live with spontaneity. And not take my loved ones for granted . . ." I paused.

Only today do I see the hypocrisy.

If you go to the University of Washington, you stay here, live at home. My mother's words echoed in my mind, like a threat. They were completely unfair to me, considering that my brother had lived at home and had such poor grades he could only get into community college and ended up dropping out at nineteen to escape to Arizona. But if I was rejected from the University of Washington and admitted into Western Washington University, she said I would go to Western and stay at the dorms there, because it was an hour and a half from her house.

My mother was a blip of oxygen that was making its way to my heart. She was an infection. And college was a pocketknife I would gladly use to dig and scrape at my flesh, because it was a small price for sweet escape. For life. And I would smile with relief when I would be rid of the infection.

When I finished my essay, I copied and pasted it into the application for Western and clicked SUBMIT. I whispered a quick prayer. Then it was time to complete my application for the second school: the University of Washington, the school that would inevitably chain me to my mother for another four asinine years. And I knew if that happened, I would be yanked underwater with the weight pulling on my ankle relentlessly. And it would not be a quick death.

I knew what I had to do. I reopened the tab for my Western Washington University application and highlighted the entire essay. I then copied and pasted it into the University of Washington application window, clicking NEXT without reading through the application. I finally hit SUBMIT. Then I waited for months.

It was no surprise that my application to the University of Washington was denied since I submitted an essay for a prompt I didn't bother to read. But the denial letter was all I needed.

"I guess I won't be living at home, Umma." I handed her my letter, grinning and attempting to hold back the excitement in my voice. I had already gotten my acceptance letter from Western Washington University. The dream of escaping my mother was becoming more of a reality. She was sitting at our dining room table when I'd shown her the rejection letter, papers scattered every which way. My eye caught a pamphlet about FAFSA and room and boarding costs. I shrugged it off.

It would be years later when I would come to learn that the reason why my mother wanted me to go to the University of Washington was not because she wanted me to stay at home to control me, but because it would have been cheaper for our family if I had lived at home and didn't pay for room and board. But of course, along with everything else my mother had kept quiet about, she didn't want me to know exactly how poor we were, despite the fact that my brother and I already knew. And without that explanation, I secretly sabotaged my chance at going to the college that would have put my family through less financial hardship. After all, there was no price too high for escaping my tiger mom.

ME NO SPEAK ENGLISH

Home life became an intolerable battlefield before I left for college; my mother and I were fighting daily. And to cope, I was drinking about four days a week. The one thing my mother didn't understand was personal boundaries. In Korea, daughters and mothers were inextricably merged into one singular identity. This was in part due to our group identity, which meant family units were perceived and felt as one identity. Individualism is very much an American ideal, whereas in Korean culture, parts were reflective of the whole. I wasn't supposed to know where my mother ended and where I began. But on a cellular level, we were splitting.

"Umma, you constantly nag at me! It never lets up—you make me feel like I'm suffocating. You have to comment on every single thing I do. Can't you give me a break?" I screamed in English.

My mother was breathing heavily, staring at me. I could tell she was trying to figure out what I was saying. She knew I was angry, because of my tone, but she had no idea what I was trying to get off my chest. Instead, she just screamed back in Korean as if I never spoke, because she couldn't address what I was saying in an impossible language.

I would revert to English when I was upset because I could barely code-switch the English in my head into the broken Korean I learned when I was a child in Korean school. And my mother never advanced my Korean vocabulary, so she spoke to me in simplistic Korean. And she kept dropping out of her English as a Second Language classes at the local community college. This decision left a severe consequence that caused a major chasm in which no one could predict the level of damage. It's something that maybe only immigrant children experience: my mother and I didn't speak the same language fluently.

If the generation gap and my Westernization weren't enough, the language barrier was turning our relationship into ash.

On top of everything else, my mother would frequently burst into the bathroom to scold me while I was sitting on the toilet. As a developing adolescent, it felt violating, partially because I was so Westernized. For my mother, she didn't understand what she was doing wrong; she came from a country where daughters and mothers bond in public bath-houses, *jjimjilbang*, and scrub each other clean while review-ing their day. Maybe part of it was because of my assault; my body never felt my own. I was never sure. But I was withering.

The summer before freshman year of college, I was fully rebelling. Every time she had something to say, it was important to me that I had the last word. I couldn't stand the fact that she coached me so matter-of-factly. My mother had determined I was an ungrateful teenager with zero life experience. The thing is, she was partly right—I didn't have any of the types of life experiences she had, but she also never had and never will have the types of life experiences I had. Not only because of the immigrant experience but also due to the sizable generation gap between us. She had me in her thirties, and she was going through menopause during my challenging teenage years, which fed our feud like kerosene on an open flame.

That summer, the blistering tension became too much; she suggested I move into my dorms early. I was shocked the suggestion came from her, but I snatched the offer off the table before she could change her mind. In no time, I was a student at Western Washington University and waiting for summer to end. I was relieved, because college was where I could mask my drinking problem.

Among the binge drinkers, I camouflaged nicely with my surroundings and no one was the wiser. Every weekend it was the same: drink to the point of blacking out completely and wake up in my bedroom. I never recalled how I made it safely home. I would also make the drive home from my college town and go from party to party, couch surfing until Monday arrived. Because I had tasted the most independence I ever had from my mother, I wanted to explore the furthest outreach of my freedom and forget that she even existed. I wanted to reinvent myself from the insecure child who hated what she saw in the mirror and feel confident in my identity and to mask the fact that I felt utterly lost. I was navigating adolescence alone, it seemed. I had no role model for womanhood, no role model to help me understand who I was and what it meant to be a freshly minted adult. My father worked all the time, and my mother never offered me any guidance; I felt like an orphan who was told to go figure out what it meant to be a woman—and further, a *Korean American* woman. My sense of self-worth was incredibly low as I began internalizing the feeling of belonging nowhere.

It was the afternoon after a night of heavy drinking, but I was still hungover and face down in a shit-stained toilet. I was holding my own hair back and miserably trying to look anywhere but inside the bowl. I was on a date at a teriyaki joint, and I had tried to eat something a little too early into my hangover.

When I glanced down, my heart stopped. The bowl was filled with blood. I quickly wiped myself up with paper towels and told my date I had to go to the emergency room. He offered to drive me.

"You're vomiting so violently, you've torn your stomach lining. Your stomach is filling up with blood," a nurse told me in disapproval. I was also severely dehydrated, so I spent the entire day in a hospital bed, hooked up to an IV. I watched bag after bag of fluid drain quickly down into the IV line and replenish what my body was desperate for.

It's so worth it, I thought. I had successfully escaped my mother, but I hadn't yet escaped myself. So I continued to drink. Drinking was the only thing I felt like I had control over in my life, so it became a way for me to cope with my anxiety toward my mother. For my entire life, she had wanted to control every aspect of me. It became, for me, similar to an eating disorder in the way that many turn to disordered eating as a way to grasp control over one's own life. But instead of binge eating or depriving my body of food, I wanted to imbibe as much alcohol as possible to make me forget ever living at home with my mother. I wanted to forget feeling like a disappointment to the one person whose approval I used to long for, while simultaneously wanting to pull away from her.

That day in the hospital, I remembered how my mother once told me about the willow and the wind. The willow that fights against the force of the wind splinters. The willow that bends to the will of the wind survives. I refused to bend, and as a result, I was splintering against my mother's will.

CHRIS HAS A SISTER?

That spring, I drove from college to my hometown to attend a wedding. Stacey, my best friend, had a sister named Jessica who was getting married. It was a rare day in Seattle's springtime when the sun was shining and the heat was palpable. The bridal party was lined up during the ceremony, which was outside the wedding venue—a charming manor that backed up to a greenbelt.

As a bridesmaid, I stood with the others in front of the guests while I tilted my face upward, then closed my eyes and felt the sun warming my face. The sky was a robin's-egg blue. The pastor was orating about the significance of "in sickness and in health" while I tuned out his droning. Stacey was crying.

The flowers in the greenbelt boasted their blooms as birds chirped in the trees. Butterflies and honeybees were floating over the clover lazily. The greenery donned blossoms like jewelry, and the grass and trees were an emerald green and glowing radiantly. I would have believed it if someone had told me I had died and gone to heaven.

Instead of Jessica's father, she had her brother, who suffered from muscular dystrophy, accompany her down the outdoor aisle in his wheelchair. As she walked down the aisle, Jessica swung her bouquet carelessly down her side like a grocery bag, instead of holding it upright. The image of her upside-down bouquet made me giggle.

And before I knew it, everyone dispersed and the bridal party was socializing with guests. We all shuffled into the manor, where there was a dance floor, a number of tables cloaked in white tablecloths, and a long table that featured an enormous roasted pig—in true Filipino style. Stacey, like the perfect hostess, was hustling around and ensuring the food was coming out in time. She wanted to make sure nothing spoiled her big sister's big day. I gave my best friend a wide berth and stayed out of her way.

The entire family was Filipino-Mexican, and because of the mute way I was raised, I could argue that I knew more about Filipino and Mexican culture than I did my own. *Lumpia* and *pansit* prompted cheerful chosen-family memories, while *kimchi-jjiggae* and *naengmyeon* prompted feelings of coldness and disappointment.

On the dance floor, Foo Fighters played over the speakers. Jessica was never going to be the conventional bride. Now that the ceremony was over, I watched her and her new husband dance. And then Jessica broke away from him for a moment to air guitar to the music. I smiled.

"Excuse me, are you Chris's sister?" The woman asking was middle-aged, plump, and had a kind face. I was taken aback.

"Yes?" I replied hesitantly, unsure how she knew my brother.

"Oh my gosh, I had no idea Chris had a sister!" After years of not talking about my brother after the night he moved away to Arizona, it was bizarre even to hear his name again.

"Chris is my son's best friend!" she exclaimed. "He used to sleep over at our house all the time growing up! Ever since he was in middle school!" I frowned. *Of course he was allowed to sleep over.*

"I'm sorry," I said, "how do you know the bride and groom?"

"Don't you know? That"—she pointed to Jessica's husband—"is Chris's best friend's wife's little brother! I'm Chris's best friend's mother! So, the groom is my daughter-in-law's brother! I know it's a lot," she said, laughing.

"Wait, I'm sorry . . . can you say that again?"

"Jessica's husband," she tried again, patiently. "That's your brother's best friend's wife's little brother." She scanned my face for recognition. "And Jessica told us all you were Chris Sung's little sister!" *But why didn't Jessica tell me all of this?* I wondered. *Why didn't she give me a heads-up?* Later, Jessica told me she assumed I knew about these connections, but that didn't take the sting out of being surprised this way.

"We just saw your brother last weekend," she went on.

"Wait . . . he came to town to visit?" I stuttered. My family and I hadn't even seen him in over five years. I felt embarrassed that I had no knowledge of anything she was speaking of. During this time, I hadn't spoken to my brother at all since that trip to Arizona, and my mother spoke to him irregularly on the phone. But she said it was because he was working so hard these days and didn't have time to call.

The kind-faced woman looked at me closely and must have realized that something was off. She was looking at me as if she'd found a long-lost friend and searched my face for answers. But I didn't know how to respond, so I just stood there as the weight of her words slowly settled down on me, like sand in water after a wave washes ashore. But the sand refused to settle.

"I really don't know, I'm sorry," was all I could manage.

"Well, anyway . . ." She seemed to want to salvage the situation, or save me from my embarrassment. "It was so nice meeting you," she said quickly, as she hurried off to her friends.

For the rest of the wedding, strangers upon strangers approached me to talk about Chris and to tell me they had no idea I existed. "Chris has a sister? He never told us!" *How could a brother hide his sister for over twenty years?*

I stood in the middle of a crowd of people, yet I was so alone and felt so exposed. I imagined this was what it would feel like if a long-lost relative was suddenly found and showed up to a family reunion. These strangers knew a part of my life that I didn't know about. They all belonged to a hidden life that my brother lived, all part of a life that lived right next door that I had no part of. He had rewritten his life and wrote me out of it.

MEEYAHN-HEH-YOH (I'M SORRY)

T he Sunday after the wedding, my mother and I were at our Korean Presbyterian church. I agreed to go with her to church to get my fill of some homemade Korean food. My visits to my parents' house were few and far between, so I wanted to take advantage. I grew up attending this church, but there were many unfamiliar faces now since I'd been away at college for a few years. Growing up, my father never joined us because he worked seven days a week—five days at the grocery store QFC and two days at Uwajimaya, an Asian seafood market, on his days off from QFC. Some days when he would come home, I would give him a big hug, bury my nose in his work shirt, and inhale deeply. I was always greeted by the smell of freshly caught fish, which I loved. I would have rather been at home, waiting for my dad to come home, than be at church with my mother.

The service ended, and I stood by the banquet table, trying to decide what to eat. You couldn't even see the surface of the table; it was crowded with plates upon plates of *tteok*, Korean rice cake. Some were rainbow-colored, firm in their texture, while others were pillowy and doughy, giving your teeth a bit of a fight to break away because they were that chewy. Some were black bean filled—my favorite. As I mulled over the options, my mother brought a friend over.

"Joan getting her English bachelor's degree!" my mother boasted.

"*Wuahhh . . .*" The woman appropriately expressed how impressed she was, her approval that I was in college (as if it were a choice in a Korean family). I tried not to roll my eyes. She then asked me a question in Korean, much more rapidly than my mother spoke to me, and I could only catch every other word. But this time, I felt prepared to respond.

I shrugged my shoulders in feigned shyness and said with fluidity, "*Meeyahn-heh-yoh . . . han-gook-mal jal moh-teh-yoh!*" The woman laughed awkwardly, and my mother's jaw dropped to the floor. The woman turned to my mother, and they chuckled at each other, and the woman walked away. My mother then descended upon me.

"Joan!" She was embarrassed because I'd told the woman I didn't speak Korean very well.

But I'd spoken the truth—and stated it with a flawless accent, might I add.

"They know I never teach you proper Korean!" And with that, she stormed off.

"Umma! But what else was I supposed to do? I don't even know how to speak to the lady!" I called after her.

She didn't reply.

Didn't she understand she had set me up to fail? Didn't she understand that if she wanted a daughter who spoke Korean fluently that she would've had to put the effort in? That you can't punish your child for not speaking the language if you didn't really understand what you signed up for when you immigrated to this country?

One of my deepest regrets was not speaking Korean fluently. I wished my mother hadn't pulled me out of Korean school. Which, in retrospect, was interesting, because she dropped out of English-speaking classes at the local community college multiple times. My dropping out of Korean school and my mother dropping out of English classes stunted us from speaking the same language fluently and truly bonding as a mother and daughter.

Did she lose hope in the two of us learning to understand each other?

I told myself speaking Korean was one of the core pillars for inclusion into a Korean community, despite the fact that there are many things that can cause feelings of rejection or displacement. What made it worse is I look the part because I am full Korean, so the expectation is that I act it. But the second I opened my mouth, I betrayed myself. It was like finding out a new handbag is a fake. When I opened my mouth, I half expected to see a label on my tonsils that read "Gucco."

What I didn't know then was that if I spoke fluent Korean and behaved like an obedient Korean daughter, I wouldn't have been Joan. Because all the crippling insecurities, and what not speaking the language meant to my identity, left me with minor trauma. And would I wish I hadn't gone through the traumas, when they were what led me to understand who I really was? It's like wishing you had a straighter nose, or in my case, wishing I had double eyelids . . . If I were any different, then would I really be me?

And if I could speak Korean, was that truly the barrier keeping me from feeling "Korean enough"? If I was realistic, my inability to speak Korean would be replaced by another barrier keeping me from feeling Korean. Because that is the thing about the Asian American diasporic experience. We're always trying to achieve perfection, when it doesn't really exist.

But none of that reasoning really provides comfort, because to this day, I still don't understand what people want when they ask me: "Do you speak Korean fluently?"

Do I? What is "fluent"?

It wasn't until my thirties when I realized that the most accurate depiction of my skill level was to give a percentage.

"I am sixty to seventy percent fluent." People seem generally satisfied with this response and leave me alone. It's much better than when kids in my youth would ask me to say phrases like a party clown.

"Go on! Say, 'Excuse me, I'm lost. How can you find the shopping mall?'"

I can't. I'd internally groan. *I'm only kinda Korean.*

DRINKING BUDDY

J essica was only able to celebrate the bliss of her nuptials for a brief moment. A few months after the wedding, I received a phone call at work. And the next thing I knew, I was standing in a church, staring at her brother's arms, which were usually resting on his wheelchair tray. But now they were pinned against his chest. His hands were turned outward, away from his body, as if trying to claw his way out of his casket before the lid was even closed. His fingers were not naturally relaxed but rigid and clutching at nothing. His eyelids were cracked open ever so slightly, and his eyes were rolled to the back of his head, milky whiteness staring back at me. *This isn't right; this isn't right! He's supposed to look like he's sleeping!* I was nineteen years old but had never experienced losing anyone to death. I tore my eyes away from his and forced myself to look at the photographs tucked around his body. I pretended like everything was normal, fully aware of the eyes among the pews, staring at my back. My guess was that the family couldn't afford a proper undertaker and, unfortunately, they got what they paid for.

The inside of the casket was inlayed with mother-of-pearl, carved in the outline of birds. It was beautiful. He would have loved it. Avoiding looking at my dear friend's face, I quickly tucked a letter I had written him near his shoulder and leaned over the casket.

Although we knew that muscular dystrophy was a death sentence to the men in Stacey's family, we'd managed to ignore it, perhaps willing ourselves to believe her brother would be spared. Peter was given until his nineteenth birthday to live, and he was thirty years old when his heart gave out in the middle of the night. Stacey's father tried to resuscitate him, but her brother was gone. We were expecting it, but we weren't prepared for it. It didn't seem that long ago that he was accompanying Jessica down the aisle at her wedding.

"Goodbye, Peter," I whispered.

I walked back to my seat in the church pew next to Stacey. I looked at her face. Stacey was drop-dead beautiful. Half Mexican, half Filipina, and tattooed from head to toe—a real tough girl. But generous when it came to giving me a place to escape to when I needed space from my mother. She had long dark hair and was a dead ringer for a Kardashian. We'd met in fourth grade, lost touch, then got back together when we were in high school because we circulated around the same party scenes. We joked that I was Kimmy from the show *Full House*; Stacey was always waking up in the morning and finding me rummaging through her fridge. I spent every weekend and summer at her house, watching TV with her and Peter while their father worked.

"Stace?" I said delicately. She stared ahead, looking almost angry, refusing to acknowledge her surroundings or even acknowledge that I was there. But I understood.

The rest of the funeral was a blur of ramblings and prayers from a pastor who looked younger than I was. I wasn't interested in insight into death from a kid who didn't even look old enough to rent a car. After the funeral, we piled into our cars to drive to the burial plot. I drove myself.

It was winter in Seattle, but thankfully it wasn't raining. I parked and walked through a field of dead grass, among rows and rows of headstones. I tucked my chin into my jacket and looked ahead to where the mourners had circled a hole in the ground. Stacey was already there, staring determinedly at the hole. Still, no tears. Eventually, the casket was lowered into the cold, damp ground, which was coated in frost like candied sugar. A blond man approached me, and I vaguely recognized him—a distant relative of Stacey's. He somberly held out a bucket toward me. I peered inside and saw dirt. I was confused. I then noticed the others throwing fistfuls of dirt into the hole in the ground. I wasn't sure of its significance, but I obediently reached in and dug my fingertips into the loose dirt, slowly closing my fist. He then moved over to Stacey. To my surprise, she shook her head. It wasn't until I saw her refuse to take a fistful of dirt when I realized what it was, what we were doing. The dirt symbolized closure. The dirt symbolized a goodbye. And when Stacey shook her head, she refused to acknowledge Peter's death. I knew that she somehow blamed herself for his death. And I knew she would plunge into drinking. But I couldn't have predicted the heavy cocaine usage to come.

In that moment, Stacey and I became fused together in our darkness, fueling each other's dependencies. Stacey was drinking to escape the pain of losing her brother. I was drinking to escape . . . well, everything. It was nice not to waste away alone. But I tried to ignore that I knew things were about to change for the worse.

ARE YOU SURE?

After Peter's funeral, I had to get back to college for classes on Monday. At this time, I had a part-time job at the mall.

One evening it was closing time. Luckily, it was one of the nights when the mall contracted professional cleaners to do a deep clean in our store. This also meant our closing duties were halved, which was a relief. The custodians arrived that night as expected, but we were still expected to sweep.

I walked to the back cleaning closet and sleepily reached up for the broom that was hanging on the back wall. Just then, I felt someone grope my rear and grunt. I whirled around and saw the custodian standing in the doorway of the closet, not two feet from me, grinning and licking his lips. He was white, middle-aged, balding, and wearing navy-blue coveralls. Without thinking, I pushed past him, and I took off running onto the retail floor. One of my managers was standing at the cash register. The other was folding T-shirts near the shelves. They both looked at me in surprise. I bolted to the register to face Sara, who was standing nearest to me.

"What is it?" she asked.

"The custodian just grabbed my ass!" I forced out in a breathless rush, as if it were all one word.

"What? Slow down! What happened?" Sara said, gasping.

The other manager slowly walked closer to us, as if in disbelief.

"The custodian," I tried again. "I walked to the back to grab the broom, and he came up behind me and grabbed me." I glanced, terrified, at the back door and wondered if he was listening.

Maryann finally decided to speak. "Are you sure?" she asked. She was still moving slowly toward us. "I mean, I want to be sure."

Sara turned to her. "Are you serious right now?"

"I know, I know!" Maryann held her hands out helplessly and began wringing them together. "But I want to be sure! I mean, what if she just made a mistake? I don't want to get him in trouble if he didn't do anything!"

Sara stared at her with her jaw open. But it was too late. Maryann's doubt became my own. *Maybe it was a mistake. Maryann is right. If I'm not sure, I shouldn't be stirring up trouble. Maybe he was reaching for something else in the closet and it was an accident.* But I couldn't get his leering grin out of my head.

"Forget about it. Just forget it," I said. Sara opened her mouth to protest, but I didn't give her a chance to say anything. "I'm not sure. I'm just not . . . I'll be right back."

Instead of finishing up my shift and helping them close, I grabbed my things and ran out into the courtyard of the mall. The mall was deserted. The iron bars were over the store entryways. Most of the lights were turned off, so I was running through darkness. All I could hear was the thudding of my sneakers hitting the floor.

I never returned for my next shift. But the damage had already been done. I had told myself that what happened in that closet wasn't a big deal. It wasn't worth getting someone in trouble for, if I wasn't sure. And I believed it . . .

. . . until 2020, when Taylor Swift released a documentary titled *Miss Americana*, when she details being assaulted by a man who grabbed her ass. *Assaulted.* I remember watching the documentary in my thirties and feeling shocked.

Assault. Never once did I consider what happened to me in the back room at the mall an assault. Taylor Swift managed to win a court case because a man had grabbed her without her consent.

That's assault?

But there was no court case for me. Police were never called to help me. I never reported it, because I didn't know I could or had a right to. The seriousness of my experience had never sunk in for me. And I didn't have anyone to tell me otherwise. I was a teenager when the janitor groped me and smiled. And I knew he smiled because he knew he'd get away with it.

As I continued watching *Miss Americana*, I felt sick. I felt sick because Maryann's question planted a seed of doubt that had taken root in my adolescence and plagued me through adulthood. I carried her doubt with me everywhere.

Are you sure?

After I was assaulted at that high school party, I would be assaulted numerous times more, by men who saw opportunities when I was at my lowest point. The predatory ones have a way of spotting the most vulnerable woman in the room: the woman who thought being drunk was the only way to tolerate herself; the woman who had just enough doubt in herself to make her the perfect target; the woman who would wake up, unsure of the night before and of the tiny voice inside her head that would ask, *Are you sure?*

And the answer would always be no. Because no one in her life validated her experiences. No one in her life told her to trust herself.

For years of my adulthood, I would be brainwashed to believe that an assaulter would know better about the boundaries of my body than I would. And how would they get away with it? I'm sure people wonder. How could one woman be assaulted so many times?

And my answer to them is: when you have been hypersexualized and fetishized so much as an Asian American woman, you learn that to survive means to sever the conscious from the subconscious. When a man would violate my body, my mind would flee. It was as if I were being hypnotized. I knew, but I didn't take notice, the same way I wouldn't notice a gnat sitting on my eyelash. But the knowledge of my body's violations pestered me beneath the surface.

A part of me also wonders . . . if I had learned earlier that what the custodian did to me was assault, if those managers had advocated for me . . . would I have continued to be assaulted?

I don't ask out of a place of blame. But at the same time, I think I know what the answer is.

And the travesty is that when Sara tried to argue with Maryann about my assault at the mall . . . I'm sure that when she was gearing up to defend me but chose to back down, she had asked herself, *Am I sure?*

WHAT WOULD JESUS DO?

Western Washington University didn't have a Greek Row. It was notorious for not having one. Students would say it was what kept Western "Western" rather than it becoming one of those Frat Row colleges with problematic behavior. But the problematic behavior was everywhere, because problematic men are everywhere.

Because we didn't have a Greek Row and our football team was embarrassingly awful, the boys' rugby team became the party gods at Western. And all the parties were at the Rugby House, a battered house with broken furniture, chipped flooring, and DIY patchwork walls.

It was Halloween 2006. I was wearing a yellow cardigan and flared jeans instead of a costume. My roommates and I were already drunk, slamming numerous Natty Ices, as we called them—the rugby team favorite. Two guys were simultaneously trying to pick me up, and I was spending the night trying to figure out which one to go home with. I was desperate for anything that resembled love.

One of the two guys came to the party dressed as Jesus. The other guy, like me, was not in costume. He was wearing a black DC hoodie and DC skate shoes, and he followed me around all night, telling me that he believed I was the love of his life. He made me feel incredible. I'd never had a healthy relationship, and this felt genuine; it felt real.

The Jesus character had gotten out of a long-term relationship in which she had cheated on him. He was looking for someone steady, who wouldn't mind going slow with him. He had shoulder-length brown hair and was kind and gentle; the way he spoke was soft. This automatically made me disinterested. The skater boy had a high and tight haircut and huge blue eyes and was ready to commit himself to me after knowing me for so little time. He was sure we were meant to be, that our meeting was destiny. He suggested we go back to his place. I didn't have to think twice. I chose to go home with the skater boy. His name was Blaine.

After the party, we went back to his house, where we immediately began having sex on his mattress, which was on the floor. His clothes and shoes were littered and scattered around the floor, and I didn't mind. Before either of us had a chance to come, I let out a moan, and he suddenly went flaccid.

"What did you say?" he whispered.

"Nothing, I said nothing." I didn't know what he was asking.

"You said 'Adam'! Who the fuck is Adam?" he demanded.

"Oh my God, I didn't say anything! I didn't say Adam!" I protested, afraid because he had started to shout.

He reached over and started rifling through his belongings on the floor. He pulled out a Glock 34. I didn't have a chance to gasp, because my breathing had stopped altogether.

He held the gun up to his temple. "If I can't have you, I might as well not even live."

I scrambled to the edge of the bed and soothingly began comforting him. "I'm not going anywhere! Please put the gun down."

"Prove it. Prove it that you care about me." He handed me his gun, and I knew what he was asking. My hand was shaking, and I held the gun up to my head. The metal felt cold against my skin.

"What do you want?" I asked quietly.

"That's enough," he said. He took the gun back. He seemed relieved. I wouldn't have thought he didn't come, the way he suddenly relaxed. He just wanted to know I was willing to pull the trigger.

We had been together for months, and I had dropped so much weight from stress, I looked skeletal. In high school, I was a size four. After being with Blaine for so long, I dropped to a size zero, and even then, my jeans fell off my bony hips.

Blaine refused to use a condom when we had sex. He would frequently rave about how much he wanted a baby boy.

"And you know he would be my whole world, right? You can't get jealous, because you'd be nothing."

I would nod in acknowledgment.

I'd squirm uncomfortably whenever he'd mention it, as I knew I'd be completely screwed if I got pregnant. And for once, I wasn't afraid of what my mother thought, but I was terrified at what would come if I was tethered to this man for life. I felt dirty, disgusting, and hopeless.

Thankfully, my roommate insisted I go with her to Planned Parenthood and get birth control and a stock of Plan B. She hated Blaine and tried numerous times to coach me into breaking up with him, but I knew I couldn't. I had too much self-loathing to respect myself enough to do it.

And as Blaine liked to remind me, "Your own mother doesn't even love you . . . you think you'll find someone other than me who will?" He knew my weakness, so he'd shove the knife in and twist the blade until I'd succumb again to be mindlessly his. And I didn't even want to be with him any longer, but I was so isolated. All of my friends hated him, and one by one, he helped me destroy my relationships with them. After he was through with them, I didn't have a friend left; he successfully cut me off so I became dependent on him. And I was just too afraid of the alternative: a life alone. So I stayed for another year of my life that I would pay all the gold in the world to have back in my pocket.

One evening, Blaine was strung out as always. He took Adderall every night, and his eyes, which I initially was so drawn into for their intensity, I now understand were not intense but constantly dilated and darting back and forth. The love bombing that I felt the first night we met was also a result of his manic energy from being on pills night after night. He wouldn't sleep for days. And he was also off his bipolar medication; he used to be on a lithium-based antidepressant and, as a result, would have incredibly high highs and incredibly dark lows. Frequently, he would pull his handgun out at parties if, God forbid, a guy ever talked to me or if someone made him look stupid. Once, while I was talking to a guy, I saw his hand flash between us, holding an Olde English forty-ounce glass bottle, which he proceeded to smash over the guy's head.

Blaine and I were watching TV that evening. His room was a disaster; nothing was organized, and everything was strewn over the carpet. It looked as though he were homeless and squatting in an empty apartment. His roommate was home in the other room. Clive was thirty years old and back in college to get his bachelor's. His girlfriend was Shannon, and she was nineteen. From the sounds of it, they were having sex in the next room.

Blaine always found a reason to call me a slut or a dirty ho. That night he found my point-and-shoot Nikon camera, which had a stored photo of me posing with my childhood friend. I had just gone home for the weekend and took photos of our time together.

"You little fucking slut! I knew it!" he screamed at the top of his lungs.

"What the fuck are you talking about?" I screamed back. I had become defiant once more. "Call me that again, and I'm gonna smash that big-screen TV of yours!" His prized possession was a sixty-two-inch TV that he had charged on his credit card and was struggling to pay off.

"Oh yeah?" he growled. And then he stepped forward quickly and wrapped both hands around my neck and squeezed. As I looked into his dilated, empty eyes, I knew that the next several seconds would determine whether I lived or died.

I dropped to my knees, struggling against him, hitting him, scratching his face. I was losing. I was choking. I was running out of air.

I only had one choice: I closed my eyes and forced my body to go limp. He released my neck, and I fell to the floor, pretending to pass out.

I didn't dare open my eyes to see what his next moves were. But I felt him grab my ankles and drag me out of his bedroom. When he dragged me through the living room, I heard his roommate's voice.

"Oh my God, what the fuck happened?"

"Dumb bitch forgot her place," Blaine replied, casually.

Blaine continued to drag me out the front door. My moment was coming. He dragged me into the front yard onto the wet grass. He dropped my legs. When he turned back around toward the house, I jumped to my feet and ran.

I ran and ran, as far as I could, without looking over my shoulder. I ran down the main roads in Bellingham, and when I came to an open place where I could clearly see that I was alone on the street, I fell and cried.

And that's when a police car pulled over.

The following moments were a blur. A flash of a camera bulb in my face. The police officers taking photos of my neck. Recounting the night so they could write it down. They loaded me in the back seat and drove me home. Before I got into my apartment, they told me they were going to his place to pick him up. They called me later that night and told me they took him to the local jail and photographed the scratches on his face.

The next morning when I woke up, I stumbled into the bathroom. The night before left me feeling like I had a bad hangover. When I looked into the bathroom mirror, I was taken aback. The whites of my eyes were completely red. He had choked me so violently that the blood vessels in my eyes had burst.

I returned to my room and dug through my belongings until I found a pair of sunglasses. I set them by my purse so I could wear them if I had to leave my apartment. Then I crawled back into bed to try to fall back asleep so I didn't have to think about the night before.

I was rattled awake by my cell phone ringing.

"Hello, is this Joan?" a male voice asked.

"Yes . . . who is this?"

"This is Blaine's legal defense. Blaine is still in a holding cell, and we want to make sure he's out soon so he can go back to his family. I'm just trying to get the whole story. Why would he do that to you? Did you maybe do something to provoke him?" the lawyer said, wheedling.

I don't know why, but in that moment, I felt guilty for threatening him, for saying I was going to smash his TV. A voice in my head said, *That's something a psycho would say. Things got out of hand because I was crazy; I escalated events.*

"Um . . . I guess I was the one who said I was going to break his TV, so he just snapped . . ."

"Oh, you threatened him with violence first?" The lawyer perked up—self-defense. I had no clue.

"Yeah . . . but, I mean, I'm only five foot five. I really can't do that much damage. I wasn't serious."

"Yeah, yeah, that doesn't matter." The lawyer thanked me, then hung up.

Several hours later, I got another phone call. This time, my phone showed his name.

"Do you have any idea what jail is like?" Blaine screamed in a high-pitched, whining voice. "I had to sleep on the fucking floor with piss everywhere, like a fucking delinquent! Where there were actual criminals! I didn't deserve this!" he moaned.

While he was crying into the phone, all I could think about was the Jesus at the Halloween party. According to my therapist, the natural decision of someone with complex trauma is to continually select partners who remind them of what they're used to—if we're used to abuse, then we pick the partner who fits the mold.

"I wish I had picked Jesus," I would say to my therapist, years later. "Now, it's such an obvious choice. The Good Boy."

My therapist shook her head. "After what you've gone through, it makes sense you'd pick the guy who'd say, 'I'm taking you home, let's go.'" She looked at me for a moment before asking, "What is the one feeling you have, now that you're looking back at all this?"

I didn't hesitate. "Shame. I feel shame."

"Really?" Her eyebrows were raised.

"Yeah. Most girls my age knew better. They didn't get themselves in abusive relationships. They had happy, normal experiences in college. They were off dating and having fun . . . I wouldn't change the way my life is now, but I just feel robbed of my youth. I can't explain it."

"But most girls didn't experience complex trauma and have a relationship with their mother like you did. 'Shame' implies that there is something wrong with you. It was a natural decision to pick what you knew—someone who made you feel like your mother did. And also . . . he weaponized what he knew about your mother to make you stay."

Your own mother doesn't love you, I recalled him saying.

Well, I guess my therapist was right.

"Have you ever seen that movie with Gwyneth Paltrow? *Sliding Doors?* I just wish I could see what the alternative was. I wish I picked Jesus." I forced a laugh, referring to the other guy at the Halloween party who was dressed like Jesus.

"Joan," my therapist said, "if you picked Jesus to go home with . . . we would have to be unpacking some other issues entirely."

I laughed. This time a genuine laugh, about a time in my life I had never laughed about before. *So this is healing*, I thought.

CRUEL SUMMERS

After the incident with Blaine, I needed a distraction. For me, college was not defined by the academic months; it was defined by the summers of stupendous numbness. When I reflected on my college years, it was a montage of drunken summers.

Against my better judgment, I decided to go camping with a group of about eight "friends" later that summer. I didn't actually know any of them that well, but my standards for being called a friend of mine were relatively low.

It took us four hours to drive to Eastern Washington, stopping along the way to buy beer. We arrived at our campsite sometime in the afternoon. We were setting up in a clearing among evergreens, but it was much drier in Eastern Washington. It was so hot—it must've been almost a hundred degrees outside, and whenever someone moved, they would kick up a cloud of dust and dirt. I felt like I was suffocating.

When dusk fell, I heard the murmur of voices in the woods, of other campers outside of our own site, the glows of their campfires ebbing among the trees. I didn't grow up camping like these other kids. In fact, this was my first time, so this was all new to me. It was odd to me to be with a bunch of strangers in the woods. And it didn't occur to me that I was the only person of color around.

Most of the group I was with was already drunk at this point. A group of girls was walking past our site, on their way back to their camping trailer, which was located right next to our spot. And a girl in our group, a friend's girlfriend I didn't know well, yelled something I didn't quite hear, but it sounded like an insult. The next thing I knew, the group of girls walked over to our site and circled me.

"We heard what you said, you stupid Chink!" one of them taunted. I was dumbfounded. As the six girls were screaming at me, I noticed that they had on headbands with springs attached, complete with little penises that were bouncing delightfully as they individually yelled racial slurs and a variety of insults in my face.

"Slut!"

"Chink!"

"Bitch!"

They were stoning me with their slurs. As I looked at their outfits and their headbands, it dawned on me that the girls were there camping for a bachelorette party.

"I didn't yell anything! It wasn't me!" But they didn't believe me. The penises continued to bounce.

"Chink! Chink!" one girl yelled repeatedly, shoving me as I stumbled in the middle of their circle. My so-called friends stayed silent and stood back to watch whatever was about to happen. I felt sick to my stomach, feeling a burning rage from head to toe. I lunged at a girl donning a bride-to-be sash, who stood at the forefront of the group, jeering at me.

"You wanna black eye to go with your wedding dress?" I shrieked. As I got closer to her, I felt arms wrap themselves around me. One of the guys I was camping with picked me up and swiftly threw me to the ground in a body slam. I felt utterly betrayed. "Do something!" I yelled at him desperately. But he stood over me, doing nothing.

The door to the girls' trailer swung open. An older woman, maybe in her forties, wearing a crop top and denim cutoffs, rushed up to me. She wore a big, curly purple wig, large-framed seventies disco glasses, and an identical penis headband like the other girls.

"Stop this! Don't fight! She's getting married!" she pleaded with me, as if I were the assailant. I got off the ground, covered in dirt, then turned on my heels and ran off. It wasn't until I was away from the group that I had a moment to be appalled at my friends' passiveness. No one had stood up for me. I was hyperventilating, choking. I felt my anger consume me. I felt nothing but heat and nausea at the first racial slur ever directed at me, and even worse, they didn't even call me by the correct racial slur: Chink is a racial slur for Chinese people. The indignity of being called the incorrect racial slur . . . I am Korean, and they didn't even know to call me a Gook. I almost laughed; it was insult on top of injury. It was a good thing that I never reached the girl, because I would've strangled her. I looked up and noticed a tree in the clearing that I had run to. I marched up to the tree and took a deep breath. I wound my arm back and released. My fist made contact with the bark, and I broke my hand.

Later that night, I drank about eleven beers to numb my physical and emotional wounds. I usually averaged about twelve. I waited in the tent, pretending to sleep. The sun had set, and the fire had died to embers while the noises in the campgrounds faded to murmurs. When I was sure everyone in my own camping party had fallen asleep, I rummaged through my duffel bag looking for something more to ease the throbbing in my broken hand. I found the plastic baggie filled with OxyContin that Stacey had given me earlier that week to give the alcohol a little kick when we drank. I tossed a few of the pills in my mouth, then swigged from an open can of beer I had in my tent. I felt restless, so I decided to go on a walk through the woods.

The chill in the night was surprising, considering how hot it had been during the day. The cool breeze felt comforting. I was wearing shorts and a tank top, and I crossed my arms, hugging myself for warmth. I walked away from my camping site, feeling the urge to get as far away from there as possible. There were no allies there, and I couldn't go home, because I'd hitched a ride with one of them. I was never known for having a sense of direction, but I didn't care if I got lost. As I continued to walk, I suddenly felt so alone. In that moment of weakness, all my insecurities came flooding in. What had happened earlier that day, the distance between my mother and me . . . I felt like we lived on two separate planets. But I needed a mother more than ever. Especially now, when I felt like a reject, an outsider. My Asian-ness felt so ugly. I felt unwanted, unloved. My self-worth had hit an all-time low, and I had no one to talk to, no one to confide in. Would anyone even miss me if I was gone? I thought about the bag of pills waiting for me back in the tent, and they began to sing to me.

I continued to wander through the woods for what seemed like hours, until I came to a road. I paused, wishing it were a busier time of night so I could jump out in front of a car. But no such luck. Across the street was a beautiful log cabin. And the lights were on inside.

I can't say what came over me, but I walked right up to the door and knocked. A beautiful blonde, blue-eyed woman answered. She was in her late thirties, early forties, and her mouth fell open in surprise. A beautiful woman, living in her beautiful log cabin. Living what I assumed to be her perfect, beautiful life.

"I'm thinking about killing myself," I blurted out.

Her eyes widened. She then did something completely unexpected. She pulled me in and hugged me. We spent the next hour or so sitting on her couch, her listening to me talk. I was so drunk and high; I had no idea what I was telling her. An accumulation of years of sadness, probably.

I heard her voice struggle to get through my mental fog: "I'm sure your mother loves you very much; suicide is not the answer," she said.

I tried to hang on to her words, but I was being pulled away, as everything quickly started to fade to black. And then, as if in the same moment, I woke up. I was staring at an orange nylon wall.

I had somehow found my way back to the tent, a miracle considering that I was blackout drunk. I stared at the bright fabric for a moment. Then I groaned at the sharp pain in my head and in my hand. My mouth felt like it was filled with cotton balls, and I began to cough. I sat up and winced. When I looked down at my hand, I saw that it had been carefully, tidily bandaged. I reached into my duffel bag and found the bag of pills, still full. For years to follow, I thought of the woman in the cabin in the woods and wondered what she could've said to save me from myself.

After that particularly cruel summer, I was determined to focus on earning money. If the camping summer wasn't depressing enough, the next summer was the cherry on top, because I had to work most days. I also had to stay sober Monday through Thursday, since being drunk at school or work was the only boundary I never crossed.

I was mainly driven by bitterness. I received various phone calls from my girlfriends from high school that they were all doing prestigious unpaid internships to get them prepared for life after college. What crossed my mind, when I tallied up what they were doing versus what I was doing, was that they were the rich kind of Asian and I was the poor kind of Asian. I was stuck working a minimum-wage nine-to-five job to afford to get by. I didn't have the luxury of working an unpaid internship.

I spent my summer working at a Rite Aid with a cast of characters who could have been in a Quentin Tarantino film. We had a Baskin-Robbins variety of customers, a good chunk of them crystal meth cookers. They always had bad acne, a result of picking their skin in response to the irritation from the fumes coming off the drugs while cooking. Miracle-Gro and Sudafed were popular on their shopping lists, and part of my training was identifying what a meth-cooking shopping list looked like, to try and discourage customers from purchasing their stockpiles.

One man strolled in every Sunday to pick up his medication from the pharmacy and to buy a pack of Depends for his mother. He had terminal cancer, and he took care of his mother, who was also reaching the end of her road. It was the first time I saw how cruel life could be, a son and a mother dying together.

Another weekly visitor had a gray mustache, always wore a faded baseball cap, and carried around a cane topped with the wooden head of a duck. He reeked of stale beer and repeatedly professed his love for cribbage. My heart broke a little bit every time I saw him, as he would always gaze upon my face, claiming I looked identical to his sister JoAnne. He was always drunk, which explained why our encounters played out the same every time, like a clip from a movie on repeat.

A character in his midthirties with jet-black hair would zoom in for his daily six-pack of Coors Light and one orange-flavored Sparks drink. Whenever we cashiers caught a glimpse of him in the window, we announced, "Here comes eighties guy." This guy looked thirty-six from a distance but fifty when he got to the register. He wore black, ripped, skintight jeans; a leather jacket; fingerless gloves; throwback high-top Reeboks; and a belt made of old bullet casings. Every day he would ask for his usual Marlboro Menthol Lights.

Rite Aid supplied cigarettes to a lot of people we should not have been selling cigarettes to. I didn't know my customers so much by name but by the names of their cigarette brands. *There's Virginia Slims . . . I haven't seen Lucky Strikes in a while . . .* I'm positive that 80 percent of our nicotine customers had lung cancer, their yellow teeth glowing over the checkout stand, their hacking coughs making me visualize tar. Several of them scrambled to pay for their addictions with sofa change and EBT cards that were frequently denied.

Among the cast I worked with at Rite Aid was a tattooed, raven-haired, middle-aged woman with alabaster skin who wore leather pants and always smelled of vanilla perfume and peppermint Tic Tacs. There was a die-hard Christian middle-aged man who referred all our homeless customers to a Christian radio hotline. And, last but not least, was a blonde mother-hen type, who ate a single Snickers for lunch every day and had a twenty-three-year-old daughter who was dying from an incurable stomach disease. Meanwhile, our manager was a man who suffered from severe eczema, so our nightly duties included sweeping the checkout stands for his flaked skin—of which there were piles and piles.

Beth was another coworker, closer to my age. I guess she was also a friend. Once, when I was leaving for a trip to Mexico, she gifted me with some antacids and a box of condoms. She was a quiet, soft-spoken girl from Arkansas, whose teeth made me think of a rabbit. She modestly held a hand to her mouth whenever she giggled. Beth was as shy and sweet as she seemed, but she was also sleeping with her boyfriend's little brother after reaching out to him on his Myspace. Beth was twenty-four, and the kid was in high school. She once had me over for dinner, and when I was helping her cook, I found her hamster in the freezer. Its stiff little carcass was wrapped in tinfoil, like a leftover burrito. Beth had written on his shiny casket with a Sharpie: *Dear Hampy, you were the best hamster ever. Love, Beth.*

And then there was me. I was the girl filled with sullenness that she had to work at a minimum-wage job she thought she was too good for—a job similar to my father's. While restocking shelves, I methodically smooshed every single candy bar as I placed it on the shelf. I wanted a customer to take it home and have their joy falter after seeing my thumbprint in their candy. And the feeling of sinking my thumb into a Russell Stover chocolate-covered marshmallow was utterly satisfying. Because I was trapped in a never-ending movie about stasis and sadness. Because I was stuck here, and my friends were not.

My junior year at college yielded: one theater professor who always had an erection when he made us do yoga to warm up, endless hangovers in class, one *ménage à quatre*, and one failed course. I had a film professor who did a cameo for *Law & Order* and *Sex and the City*, which left a gaggle of girls following him around the gym to watch him lift weights. And I had a paid homework assistant, which was a friend I started paying to do my math assignments because I was having trouble passing math.

The year was a blur. I was struggling to make it to my classes, not because of drinking but because of something else that I never knew I should have paid closer attention to: I was struck with serious insomnia. I would find myself utterly exhausted in the middle of the day, but when it came to the night hours, I wouldn't sleep a wink. In fact, I would lie in bed and manically think about various memories that I wished I could relive and redo. I would overthink and overanalyze every moment that didn't sit well with me—a stomachache of the mind. I was overindulging on unhealthy thinking patterns and negative self-talk. It got to the point that my theater professor dropped my grade an entire letter because my attendance became so unpredictable.

I was relieved when summer arrived and my sleeping patterns wouldn't affect my grades. And this was my last summer at college, my last summer with yet another odd job to help make ends meet. I was working at a call center that performed surveys over the phone to collect data for health companies. *How satisfied were you with your recent health clinic visit? Very satisfied, satisfied, or dissatisfied?* I was told to go jump off a cliff and kill myself on my first day. Everyone assumed we were telemarketers. Like every summer, my classmates from high school were doing more interesting and productive work than I could ever do. Friends were moving onto bigger and better internships at large companies, like Microsoft and General Mills cereal. These were internships that you actually took a plane to get to, internships where you actually lived in another city for the summer to gain job experience. They were adding to their résumé to be more desirable candidates after they got their college degrees, while I was adding "Rite Aid cashier" and "glorified telemarketer" to mine.

One afternoon, after having convinced a man to answer the health-care questionnaire over the phone, he asked me, "Where are you from?"

"California." I knew he couldn't see my face, but the question was familiar, one that plagues Asian people in a specific and irritating kind of way.

"No, I mean, what nationality are you?" the voice on the other end asked.

"Korean. I'm Korean," I said, wondering where this was going.

"Oh, wow! You speak English so good. You sound Aryan!" I didn't know what he meant by that, so I responded how I thought I was supposed to.

"Thank you." It sounded like a compliment.

Why would he think to ask me this question when he can't even see my face? I wondered. But then my question was answered when he explained his recent encounter with a telemarketer.

"You know, if we're going to have people answer phones, they should be able to speak English. Last week, I spoke to some Indian person, and I couldn't even understand what they were saying—their accent was so thick! If you're going to live here, you gotta speak English."

"Yes, sir."

Later that night, I googled "Aryan."

I began to notice an emergent pattern of people in society complimenting people of color for their ability to appear as "white" as possible. Or maybe, more accurately, as "un-foreign" as possible. I didn't understand until years later that the man on the phone hadn't given me a compliment but was contributing to the problem of people of color being told that to show any sign of being different was never a good thing. I never questioned the utter contradiction that I would be perpetually treated as an outsider in this country despite the fact that I was American. Even if I had a "foreign" accent, even if I wore a hijab, whatever identity I presented in society would have to be American in nature, because I was American. For now, I was only keenly aware of my Korean identity, which, to me, had no place here and was something to be ashamed of, something to disguise.

ASIANS ARE STUDIOUS

I declared my major in English language and literature, with an emphasis in creative writing. Since writing had always been my passion, it was relatively easy for me to get decent grades to pass all my courses despite drinking to the point of blacking out every weekend. Besides, every great author had a drinking problem anyway, I reasoned. For my degree, I had to fulfill a prerequisite in the arts, so I registered for Music History.

My professor was a stout middle-aged man with gray hair and a beard to match. He wore a tweed jacket with leather elbow patches. His silver spectacles perched on the tip of his nose as he spouted off about Tin Pan Alley and his time as part of the Bill Evans Trio (which, at the time, I had no idea was actually a big deal). I could not have drawn a more professorial-looking man if I had tried. He usually tilted his face toward the ceiling, dreamily reminiscing about times past. There was something about his nostalgia that spoke to me; I, too, felt as though I was nostalgic. But instead of dreaming about the past, my head was usually in the clouds, dreaming about the future so I could escape the past.

We were expected to show up to class and take copious notes on the lecture, and every single thing out of the professor's mouth was fair game for the tests. I had never had a professor teach in this format. Even a metaphor in a rant could show up on the quizzes. Long verbal instruction may as well have been in a different language. I struggled to take notes on the lectures, and before I knew it, it was time for the final.

The morning of the test, I walked into the expansive auditorium where the lectures were held, while other students trickled in with me. There were almost two hundred students in this class, and some had arrived early to review their notes before the test. I felt sick to my stomach. I knew I was ill-prepared. Although I had quickly reviewed my notes the night before, they were unhelpful, as they were fragmented and lacked context. When I sat down to fill in my Scantron bubble sheet, I rushed through the questions as quickly as possible, hoping the first answer that would pop into my head would be some type of subconscious recall. There were five minutes left on the test, and I suddenly realized my grave mistake: I had somehow skipped over some answers, intending to return to them, but then began filling in the wrong rows, so they no longer correlated to the correct questions. My eyes felt hot. I slowly got up out of my seat and walked down the steps to approach my professor. He looked at me curiously. I began to cry.

"Professor, I filled in my bubble sheet wrong, and now I'm out of time. The answers aren't lined up to the right questions, because I wasn't paying attention," I blubbered. He looked at me like a grandfather would look at a child who had just experienced an injustice at school.

"Oh dear. Don't cry. We'll make this right," he soothed. I was utterly surprised at his warmth. "How about I just give you an A?" he whispered.

Stunned, I could only manage an "Oh!"

"We both know you would've gotten all of them right," he said, winking. I forced a smile, thanked him, and returned to my seat. I couldn't believe what had just happened. But instead of feeling lucky, I felt ashamed, because I knew I would've failed that test. I felt like a fraud, an impostor. But I didn't realize then why he looked at me, the most anonymous student in his enormous class, as a student who would have gotten an A.

So, when people ask me to explain what "model minority myth" is, it's a difficult response for me to reconcile. Those who are very well-versed in model minority myth understand the crushing implications of a society that expects all Asians to be high performing, while ignoring how colorism impacts our communities, and ignoring the implications on our mental health. And society expects us to be superficially successful in academics and careers with few resources, even when we desperately need them (especially those of us who come from immigrant families or are low-income). But it's actually moments like these, getting an undeserved A on my college final, that I find difficult to explain.

Because what we don't want to advertise too loudly is that it also comes wrought with privilege. Getting a "pass" without a second thought, for being a light-skinned East Asian, means that sometimes you do get privileges. But we don't want to discuss these moments too loudly, because it has enough weight to counteract all the advocacy work in dismantling the model minority myth for those whom it harms the most. It has enough for people to say, "Look! You got an A without even studying! And you're really going to convince me that you are a victim of racism and discrimination?"

And that is the complexity of the Asian American experience. Without understanding the idea of multiple truths, the general public will never understand us.

Is it possible to get privileges as a light-skinned Asian American? Yes.

Is it possible that Asian American women are disproportionately impacted by sexual assault by white men? Yes.

Is it possible that your teacher will have higher standards for you in the classroom? Yes.

Is it possible that you are expected to perform, but when you show signs of depression and anxiety, you will be ignored? Yes.

Is it possible that an Asian woman will be expected to be meek and submissive? Yes.

Is it possible that an Asian woman will be expected to be a freak in bed? Yes.

Yes.

Yes.

Yes.

CRAZY RICH ASIAN

The week after finals, my brother called but not to check in on how my exams went. No, my brother's wellness checks were a bit . . . different.

"You're still working at that piece-of-shit job?" my brother asked me, unable to hide his condescending tone. After word got out that his sister made her debut at his best friend's brother-in-law's wedding, the jig was up. He began calling my mother and me somewhat regularly to pretend that he never meant to hide his visits home. I let it slide, and I never told my mother. After years in Arizona, my brother worked as a successful mortgage broker, and I was just trying to survive college. Last I heard, he made $40,000 in one month. *How is this fair?* I thought. He should have been the black sheep of the family. He dropped out of community college at nineteen and was always getting in trouble, while I went to a traditional four-year college like my parents wanted. But he was the pride and joy of the family.

"How much do you make?" my brother asked. I mouthed the question along with him, because it was always the same. My brother spoke in price tags. His Rolex watches, his Gucci wallets, his mansion in the same neighborhood as a certain A-list celebrity . . . money, money, money.

Immediately after hanging up on my brother, I called my mother. I told her what he said, because I was feeling frustrated being the family failure. She promptly made excuses for him because of the way his childhood was. I told her how I was constantly stressed about money, especially when I saw how lavishly my friends lived and how I was the "poor one."

She reminded me in Korean: "When you see the luxuries people have, you are not seeing the money they have but the money they do not have."

I wondered what fortune cookie she got that from.

Growing up poor with your sibling makes you close—until it doesn't. When my father started working at the grocery store, our income became stable and our day-to-day life more comfortable. What this meant was that my brother lived poor longer than I did. So he got to witness our family come into a little more wealth as my father got a steady job and saved most of their money. As a result, my parents could buy me things that they could never buy him when he was my age, like a new wardrobe at the beginning of the school year. That created resentment. He never hid the fact that he thought I was spoiled, and I didn't blame him, after what my mother told me next over the phone.

"Joan, try to understand your brother. To him, money is survival. That is why he will always be obsessed with earning money." Her voice became heavy and thick with emotion as she began her story—my brother's story.

She told me about a time when my brother was in sixth grade, and she wanted to treat him to a back-to-school shopping trip at the mall. Our family was struggling, so she thought she could just charge the whole trip on her credit card. She described the day as exciting, my brother so eager to wear his new clothes to school. But at the end of their shopping trip, they arrived at the last store, and the credit card was declined. So my mother had no choice but to return to every single store they had shopped at, and my brother watched my mother return every single item she purchased for him. The credit card was to be used for emergencies only, since we were barely living within our means. When my mother maxed out the card, she didn't realize how low the limit was. As soon as the card was declined, she knew she needed to return everything so there was credit for a true emergency—something she had forgotten until she wanted to spoil her son for his first day of school. All the while, my brother was reassuring my mother that he didn't really want the clothes. My mother finished talking and was quietly sobbing on the phone.

My heart was in a million pieces. I saw my brother as that child, frozen in time. I decided to just let that child hate me if that's what he needed. Everyone needs somebody to blame for their misery. Now that I understood my brother, I began to let that relationship go.

When I told my brother I was thinking about joining the military after college, he asked, "Would you make good money?"

"No," I said without apology.

"Then why the fuck would you join?" he asked. To him, it was a rhetorical question.

I finally graduated college in December of 2008. And I graduated early, because every quarter I took an extra-large credit load. I wanted to graduate as quickly as possible, to avoid being a leech on my family's finances since my parents were helping me with housing.

What I did not anticipate was that once I graduated, I had to move back home with my parents because, with an

English degree, I couldn't get anything other than a minimum-wage job. No one had told me that you should pick a major that can help you obtain a job—you're not actually supposed to study something just because you're passionate about it. Passion doesn't pay the bills. I returned home, my tail between my legs, and I was under my mother's roof and trapped once again. And so, the cycle of drinking and staying out of the house as much as possible kicked back into high gear. There was nothing that could have made me feel less of an adult and more infantilized.

Later that summer, I found myself quite literally trapped. I was huddled in a bathroom at Alex's house, with about eight of my friends, including Stacey. When I returned to my hometown, Stacey and I were inseparable again.

"They've surrounded the house," I heard someone whisper in the bathroom. I couldn't believe I was going to have to tell everyone I got arrested. I was drunk, but I wondered if there was any way I could talk my way out of this and appear sober.

After Peter's death, Stacey and I clung to alcohol like our lives depended on it. But Stacey had a worse time of it—snorting cocaine, and crushed-up painkillers and antianxiety pills. And, similar to my assault, I knew but did not notice that she had started cutting her wrists with a razor blade. We were now drinking on most days of the week, but I reassured myself that I wasn't an alcoholic, because I didn't start my day with a drink.

You could hear our hearts beating in that bathroom, it was so quiet. And then we heard the heavy footsteps coming down the hall. Alex and I made eye contact. He was a tall, heavyset Mexican guy with scruffy facial hair. *What did you do?* I mouthed. He put a finger to his lips. I closed my eyes.

Thud, thud, thud. Someone pounded on the bathroom door.

"Police! Open up!"

We didn't respond. *Crash*—the sound of the door being kicked in. Someone grabbed my arm and pulled me into the hall, where a gun was pointed at my face. "Put your hands up where I can see 'em!" I threw my hands up, where they stayed as I walked down the hall, which was now lined with police officers. We marched and looked down the barrels of several guns. *Alex, what did you do?*

When we got outside, I counted four cop cars in the cul-de-sac. We were separated into small groups, and a police officer spoke to each of us. I looked to the curb, where Alex was being arrested. To my shock and admiration, he was laughing and cussing at the cops, yelling, "Pigs!" and spitting on the ground. One officer directed my group to put our faces down on the hood of his car. I could feel a surge of panic in my chest. If my mother could see me now.

I gingerly bent over the hood of the car and placed my cheek on the metal. I looked at my friends' faces. They looked terrified—panicked. Stacey looked pissed but unwavering, as if she knew her fate and that she had to accept it.

And even then, at such a young age, I knew the power I had when it came to managing law enforcement—the number of times I had been pulled over for speeding and talked my way out of a ticket, the number of times I had been caught drinking underage at a party and an officer let me walk away scot-free. Undoubtedly, my Asian face was kind of a get-out-of-jail-free card. As a light-skinned Asian American woman, I knew the way I was perceived: harmless. Of course, this would come back and take vengeance on me later, as I would quickly learn that when you are expected to be harmless, you are punished tenfold when you do not fulfill expectations. And I was not so harmless. I was loudmouthed, opinionated, assertive, and defiant.

I knew, in that moment, that I had to wrangle my privilege and take advantage in order to protect my friends. Stacey had an arrest record. I had to get us out of there before they ran our information. The officer who was detaining us walked over to the driver's side of his vehicle. It was then I took a deep breath.

"Sir," I began, "we don't have anything to do with this. We don't even know what's going on."

"No?" He raised a brow. "You weren't harboring someone who had multiple warrants out for his arrest?"

"No! We don't even live here! We just came for a party!" I looked at my three other girlfriends, who were nodding in agreement. Stacey was staring hard into the distance and disassociating.

"Then why'd you hide?"

"With all due respect, sir, if you knew there were cops coming with guns, I think anyone would run." The adrenaline running through my veins gave me sudden clarity to talk my way out of the situation. The cop didn't reply and told us to get in the back of his car.

"Give me an address where I can drop you girls off for the night. You need to stay put, though," he warned us. "Just for the night." We promised we wouldn't leave.

Alex ended up going to jail that evening, and I never saw him again. And Stacey . . . Stacey dodged a bullet, so to speak. But I was so ignorant about how to support someone who was grieving that I couldn't give her the support she needed. I was too naive to realize that she didn't need protection from the cops; she needed protection from herself.

THE BOOMERANG GENERATION

I had been out of college with a bachelor's for two years, and I still didn't have a sustainable job. I hadn't done any prestigious internships like my high school friends, so I had no real career prospects, since I had zero on-the-job experience, which was required by almost every single job posting.

I was sitting on the bed in my childhood bedroom and looking through the newspaper. *How am I supposed to get experience if every entry-level job requires experience?* I groaned as I looked over yet another job listing in the newspaper, crumpled it up, and threw it as hard as I could against my wall. I began hitting my head against the wall, since that felt better than thinking about my failures.

Because the economy had crashed in 2008 and was still recovering, many other college graduates like me were finding that no one was willing to hire us. The wave of retirees who were supposed to make way for us and leave a deficit in the hiring market chose not to retire during a recession. Meanwhile, my parents had sold me the American dream without any real context for what else I was supposed to do to set myself up for success. America didn't just hand jobs out once you had a college degree, contrary to their belief. And since my parents never experienced this, once again I was left navigating it alone.

I was panicking. I wasn't expecting to move back home with my mother after college, and the media was calling us the Boomerang Generation for trying to survive the recession by moving back in with parents. The only jobs accessible to me were customer-service jobs that didn't pay enough for me to live on my own, or even with roommates. I was growing exceedingly desperate. Teaching was the only viable option for someone with an English language arts degree, but I didn't get a teaching certificate, so that was not an option.

Now that I was back under my mother's roof, she tried to instill a curfew on me even though I was in my early twenties. She was still vying for control. After one night, when she had cut up my food and tried to spoon-feed me like a baby, I knew something had to change.

I ignored her curfew night after night, and she quickly became enraged at the lack of respect. Once again, I turned to alcohol to feel release, since I felt smothered at home. Until one night I came home drunk, and she tried to hit me. I stood, towering over her five-foot frame, when she realized that I had become too old to hit.

"You hit me again, I'm calling the cops," I said firmly in English. But this time, she understood every word. That was the last time she ever laid a hand on me.

It was the January I was about to turn twenty-two years old. I was intensely depressed; I was sleeping all day and all night. I knew I was in danger of losing my job because I kept calling in sick. I didn't have any sick leave left, but I didn't care—my mother was encroaching on every bit of personal space I had, one time even rifling through my purse and demanding me to explain my birth control pills.

Silently, I was seething. *Don't you know what these pills mean to me? Don't you know they were my saving grace when my boyfriend was emotionally and physically abusive? Don't you know I'm still alive because they kept me from having a baby with a monster?*

She, like many Americans, have no idea the impact that organizations such as Planned Parenthood have had on abuse victims—how, when we had no one else, they provided us with protection.

Not to mention, I was shocked my mother even knew what birth control pills were, since she'd not once had a conversation with me about birth control options.

Nothing of mine belonged to me. I yearned for independence, yet I was treated like a child. And there's nothing that tears a soul in two like not being treated your age, because when you are infantilized, there are parts of you that stay childlike. Your mind is a confused place, as it struggles to reconcile how you are actually supposed to behave. That year, I knew with clarity that I wouldn't make it past twenty-two if I didn't do something drastic to ensure my escape. I knew that I would either wind up dead at a party from alcohol poisoning, or I would end up killing myself.

In my mind, my two choices were either to join the police academy or the military. One day that January I drove to the courthouse downtown and went inside and asked a law-enforcement officer patrolling the entryway how to join the police academy. They said they weren't sure where the nearest precinct was where I could get my questions answered, but that I could look it up online.

I still hadn't made up my mind. I walked out of the building into the chill of that winter morning. I stood at the steps in front of the courthouse, and I looked up at where the most prominent dome of the courthouse building touched the gray sky.

What is to become of me? I wondered.

What am I to become?

Is it too late for me?

Then the most frightening question of them all: *Am I capable of starting a new life alone?*

As I stared out at the courthouse building, I could see my breath in the cold.

"Alone or dead," I said firmly with resolve. I reached into my purse for a coin.

Heads is military. Tails is cop.

I flipped the coin, and the coin landed on heads. *Military it is, then.*

Immediately after the coin flip, I drove to the military recruiter's office in Tukwila, Washington. When I realized that joining the military was a way for me to move out of my parents' house, while law enforcement meant I might still have to stay at home, I knew I had made the right choice. Because I wanted to eject out of this life, like a pilot escaping a nose-diving plane.

Having a place of your own is a Western idea to its core, but multigenerational households are actually common in most Asian countries. But I wasn't Asian in that way. I measured myself against the American standard of success, and I was a failure if I still lived at home.

After I signed my contract and officially joined the military, I dreaded going home and telling my mother what I had done. I knew my father would understand. My mother got over the shock quickly. She was slightly regretful, like she wished I hadn't, but I was surprised that she mostly understood, as she knew I was struggling to find a serious job. My father, on the other hand, was beaming with pride at my bravery to serve my country.

Later that week, I got a call from the recruiter's office. They said that they got a phone call from DC that they needed to send a federal agent to interview me face-to-face.

"Why?" I asked. "Does everyone have to do this?"

"Don't worry," my recruiter reassured me. "It happens sometimes. Usually, they see something that could be suspicious on your background check, so they fly someone out to check you out and give you a chance to explain what's on there."

During this time, I was working at a local movie theater—ultimate humiliation for what I thought was expected of an Asian American with a bachelor's degree. The federal agent called me for a date, time, and location. The next week, he texted my cell phone and told me that he saw a café near the theater and that he would be waiting there until my lunch break to interview me. When it came time for lunch, I walked over. We sat down, and the man—tall, middle-aged, and bald—eyeballed me up and down, scrutinizing me. Then he relaxed in his seat.

"So, this isn't uncommon that we come out and interview potential service members. Something came up on your background check, on your record, that we'd like you to explain."

I was confused. I had never been in trouble with the law, had never been arrested.

"Do you remember an incident in 2009? Maybe a run-in with the cops?" he asked.

"But I've never been arrested . . ." I stammered.

"No, not an official arrest, but maybe something they felt was worth adding to your record?" he inquired.

The incident at Alex's house. The hiding in the bathroom, the guns . . . It all came back to me in a single flash.

"Well, um . . . one time I was at a friend's house when there was a raid . . . He had multiple warrants out for his arrest, and I was at his house. My girlfriends and I were there for a party. But I wasn't arrested."

"Ah." The agent knowingly nodded his head. "So that would be something that would come up in your record, but wouldn't be an arrest. Is there anything else that happened?"

"No, that's it," I said. The agent appeared to be satisfied with my answer.

"Like I said, this is pretty standard to send someone like me out. You see, in DC, they're just guys in an office. They don't really have much to go off of when they see something like this pop up on a background check. So they send me out to check you guys out . . . you understand."

This did not feel like an interview. In fact, I kept feeling like I was waiting for it to begin. He gave me the distinct impression of a kind father, and he believed everything I said so readily, rather than giving me the interrogation I was expecting.

"So is there anything else you need to ask me?" I asked hesitantly, preparing to convince him I was not a criminal. I worried that maybe the interview hadn't even begun yet.

"Nothing, now that I look at you. See, looking at you here now, it's pretty obvious that you look harmless," he said, as he gestured to my face.

"I'm sorry . . . ?" I began, confused. It then hit me. *Oh.* I'd just been racially profiled as an obedient, law-abiding

Korean girl. I felt conflicted. I felt . . . grateful? That someone assumed innocence? That I could get the benefit of the doubt based on my appearance, on the color of my skin. But it also felt morally wrong that while others were penalized based on their looks, I was getting a pass on my background check.

In that moment, I couldn't have known that his assumption, that I was an obedient Asian girl, would work against me in the years to come, when I'd find my voice to advocate for myself. Later, when I found that voice, and people would insist that Asians were never victims of racism, I'd count up all these incidents and turn them over in my mind. It was true that these situations were wrought with privilege. But I was being subjected to racism while getting just enough "benefit" so that society could deny it.

ME LOVE YOU LONG TIME

D espite the interview with the federal officer, nothing dampened my eagerness to leave for the military. At that point, I had six months before I was leaving for basic training, more commonly known among civilians as "boot camp." I had a single credit card in my name with an $8,000 limit. My goal was to max it out before I left. Most of the balance was taken up by alcohol. It wasn't unusual that I would close my tab out with a $100 bill: eight dollars a pop, plus tip, which adds up to about ten cocktails. My alcohol tolerance was that of a rhino.

I took a $1,500 cash advance and gave it to Stacey's dad to let me live at their house for those months before I shipped out, to reduce the amount of time I had to spend with my mother. I gave the money directly to Stacey, and in retrospect, I'm not sure he ever got it. The week before I left for basic training, I had to move back in with my mother, and Stacey would borrow the last of the money in my bank account and disappear without a trace.

But before that, I found myself sitting on the floor in Stacey's bedroom one day, looking through the classified ads in the newspaper for a job, when I saw a large picture of a cartoon girl sitting in a martini glass. "Looking for beverage servers!" the ad read. And then, in fine print, it read, "Must be over 18." *That's weird*, I thought. *The legal age to work in Washington State is sixteen; why do you need to be eighteen?* I had no idea that you had to be eighteen to beverage serve, but luckily, I was in my twenties, so it didn't affect me either way. I was interested in the job, so I called. The woman was eager for me to come in and interview. But beforehand, she wanted to ask me one screening question: How was I at handling belligerent customers? To which I enthusiastically told her I was a pro.

"Oh yeah?" the girl said. It sounded like she had a huge wad of bubble gum smacking in her mouth. "Do you mind working at a gentlemen's club?"

"Er . . ." I was caught off guard. I'd heard that term before, but I didn't exactly know what it meant. I needed money, so I didn't ask for clarification. I blurted, "No! I'd love it!" All I could think about was my bank account balance. She gave me the time and place of the interview, which happened to be the next day in North Seattle, and I agreed to meet her there. I had an odd sense of commitment once I agreed. Somehow the deal was already sealed in my mind, and it was just a matter of getting there and telling them in person.

I was staring at breasts—hundreds upon hundreds of breasts. The walls of the double-wide were plastered from floor to ceiling with porn and *Playboy* centerfolds. It was probably an attempt to use these photos in lieu of wallpaper to conceal exposed pipes or any other noncompliant building conditions. I had never seen so many breasts at one time. Some of the centerfolds had autographs, and it struck me how many of these porn models and stars had visited this place.

"Um, excuse me, miss?" I asked hesitantly.

"Yeah, Rhonda," she responded absentmindedly, without even looking up from her papers. Her Frito-chip-length nails pawed away at the papers. The woman was popping her bubble gum loudly, her mousy brown hair pulled back in a messy bun. I guessed she was the same woman I'd spoken to on the phone the day before. She was wearing a dingy hoodie sweatshirt and jeans. My nose picked up on lingering cigarette smoke. *Get. Out. Of. Here!* my brain screamed.

"Rhonda, is this job for . . . a strip club?" I asked weakly.

"Gentlemen's club," she corrected me. I closed my eyes and groaned internally. "It's for beverage serving," she added, as if that made her offer any better.

In my mind, stripping was the gateway to porn. And the gateway into stripping was beverage serving in a strip club. *Oh God, was I going to be a stripper?* I began to panic. There was no way I could survive my mother's judgment if I became a stripper. *What would she tell her friends?* Given that my conservative mother's version of the sex talk was "protect your jewel," I couldn't imagine her reaction if I worked at a strip club. Despite the fact that I was embarrassingly sheltered and naive at twenty-three due to my mother's parenting, I had taken a sexual-deviance course in college. In the course textbook, there was a chapter on the stigmas around stripping. When I read this section, I was engrossed in the real world behind stripping, where exotic dancing was depicted as more empowering than shameful: there was a case study where a number of women stripped to be sex positive and to liberate themselves from society's stringent double standards around women. And much to my surprise, there were women who chose to strip in order to gain control over their sexual-assault trauma, something that I could relate to. But in this moment in the double-wide, I felt as though stripping was too illicit, because I couldn't stop thinking about how my mother would see it. My focus returned to Rhonda, who was still explaining how to apply for the job.

"I want you to go home tonight and fill out an online profile for our website. The recruiters will contact you after. Remember, the most important part is the photograph, okay?"

"Okay," I said, nodding. Well, maybe I'd at least do that, since the reality was that I didn't have any way to make money . . .

Later that afternoon, I got on my computer and navigated to the website Rhonda told me about, and I uploaded a photo of myself and created my application profile. I leaned back in my chair and thought about how badly I needed cash. I picked up my phone and called my friend Amber to tell her what was happening, and without judgment, she suggested we go to a strip club to see what it was like. I drove to her house that night to pick her up, and we drove together to downtown Seattle, home to some of the biggest strip clubs around.

As we walked down the street, it wasn't long before we found a club, and we quickly paid the cover fee to enter. The music was thumping, and the room was dim, save for the glow of neon lighting. My eyes immediately locked on the stage. A Filipina girl was on her knees, bouncing her bare breasts with her hands and sticking her tongue out. The crowd of men was going wild, and bills were fluttering onto the stage. She looked at me and winked. I blushed. Meanwhile, Amber wandered away, looking for seats for us.

"Where are you from?" A man had walked up to me without me noticing. He was white and about forty. That question again.

"California."

"No, like, where are you *from?*" he tried again.

I sighed. "I was born here," I said stubbornly, refusing to look at him.

"Like . . . what country is your family from?" He was persistent. But he was improving.

So I gave in. "Korea."

"North or South?"

I rolled my eyes. To me this question was a thinly veiled attempt to further categorize me: *Are you the good kind or bad kind?* My favorite response was that a lot of us have North Korean blood because it used to be one country. This question was like asking what part of the States your family was from when the Civil War happened. But at the same time, I was also frustrated that the default was assuming I was from a Communist country; it was like assuming I would be a foreigner since being an American-born citizen was too far-fetched.

I wasn't going to satisfy him with a real answer, so I said sarcastically, "Well, do I look like I escaped Communism to be here?"

He then studied my face. "You look so young . . . Asians are so hot."

I gagged in response and turned on my heels to walk toward the stage, where Amber had settled down. I took a seat and turned my head around to observe the beverage servers behind us. Was this truly what I wanted to do? Someone then collapsed into a chair next to me. Much to my surprise, it was the Filipina girl from the stage.

"Woo!" she exclaimed. "I'm exhausted!" I couldn't help but stare at her. She was gorgeous, tan, and had flawless skin. Her long ebony hair flowed down past her shoulders. "I just wanted to say hi."

"Hi!" I leaned over, trying to call out over the deafening music as another dancer came onstage.

"Look—have you ever thought of doing this?" She waved to the stage.

I gave her a forced grin, then pulled a face.

"Okay, I know what you're thinking, but you can make a *ton* of money because you're Asian. We're really hard-pressed for Asian girls right now, and Asians make almost double the amount the white girls do." *Maybe you're hard-pressed because they're all thinking about their crazy conservative mothers*, I thought. A tall, meaty bouncer wearing a suit approached, until he was standing over us.

"Did you tell her?" He looked to the Filipina girl. She nodded.

"Seriously," he said, "we could really use some more Asian girls. The guys love it." He held out a business card, and I took it.

"I'll think about it!" I shouted over the noise. I slipped the card in my pocket. And I did think about it—for days. But the mere thought of my mother disowning me prevented the card from ever resurfacing from my pocket. And I wrote off the idea of beverage serving, out of fear of what my mother would say, despite the fact that I found the offer and the money extremely tempting.

The day after the strip club, Stacey and I were on the way to another party and I was telling her all about the night before. We were in stitches from laughing so hard. We were in her eggplant-colored Mitsubishi Eclipse, her prized possession. She suddenly pulled into the parking lot of an ampm convenience store.

"What are you doing?" I asked.

"Just a quick errand," she responded dismissively.

She reached behind my seat and grabbed her purse. Then she pulled out a small plastic baggie of white powder. I stayed quiet. I suspected as much, but I didn't want to know. I watched as she used her pinkie nail to scoop a small amount of cocaine and lift it to her nostril. She sniffed and sighed. She dipped her pinkie back into the bag as I looked away. I couldn't explain why I felt disappointed, since I wasn't technically sober and couldn't say no to a drink.

Then a car pulled into a spot by the gas pump behind us. Stacey quickly looked in her rearview mirror. She swiftly twisted the baggie in her hand and sniffed repeatedly. She closed the bag into her fist and opened her car door.

What is this? I thought, panicked. I watched Stacey from my seat as she walked confidently up to two guys. She seemed to argue with them for a moment, and I heard her yell. She turned around and came back into the car, where I felt myself release the breath I had held when she walked outside.

"They just accused me of snorting their cocaine!" She laughed derisively.

I looked at her, taken aback. *That's because you did!*

"I just told them, 'You want me to tell my dealer what you just said?' Then I told them if they didn't believe me, they can measure it! And they backed off!" She laughed at her own bluff, her own cleverness.

I said nothing. And it didn't matter. Stacey was high and acting in a way that made me feel as though she were sitting in that car alone. She lost sight of me, in more ways than one. When the radio played Tupac, she shouted, "I love this song!" and cranked it up.

I looked carefully at my friend's profile, just as I did the day we buried her brother.

"Stace?" I said gently. She didn't hear me. I tried again, shouting this time. "Stace!" She said nothing.

As I looked at her face, I looked down the path she was on and realized, sadly, I couldn't follow her there.

The following week Stacey called me. She was hysterical, as her beloved Eclipse was in the impound lot. They wanted $400. I checked my account online and saw that I had about $120 in my checking account, and I was leaving for basic training in two weeks.

"It's not enough, but I'll give you what I have. Promise me you'll pay me back before I leave. This is the last of my money, and I need to be able to get by until then."

"I swear," she promised.

She stopped picking up my calls.

The week before I was leaving for basic training, my phone rang: an unknown number.

"Hello?" I asked tentatively, hoping it was Stacey.

"Hi, is this Joan?" The voice on the other end was male, deep, and theatrical. "Look, I'm Bennie. I own Showgirls in Seattle, along with all the major clubs in the city."

I pictured James Gandolfini from *The Sopranos* on the other end of the phone. I must've driven by Showgirls a million times. Who hadn't? They had a huge billboard with neon legs crossing and uncrossing.

"I saw your profile online. I want you to come strip for me. Forget about beverage serving." The online profile! I had forgotten after all this time that the profile was still active.

"I'm flattered, really, but I can't. I joined the Air Force, and I leave next month."

"Well, if you're ever back, then!" he insisted.

"Sure, okay." I indulged him. "I'll think about it." He continued to ramble on, trying to make his offer more tempting. But I wasn't listening.

This wasn't the first time I'd experienced being fetishized for being Asian. I honestly didn't know what to make of it, but I began feeling weary and suspicious of strangers who wanted something from me. When I started dating in college, every white boy I ever dated was accused by his friends of having "yellow fever," because Asian women were fetishes and not actual people. Not to mention the sexual mythologies around Asian women; when I was old enough for the bars, white men came up to me randomly and asked me if I had a sideways vagina, which would have been almost laughable if they weren't seriously asking. It was clear they had never opened a biology textbook in their lives. At parties, drunk white men asked me if I gave happy-ending massages. Guys feigned interest in dating me only because they wanted to see what it was like to have sex with an Asian girl. These same men, I would discover, frequently had girlfriends or wives that they would have no qualms about cheating on, just to see if sex with an Asian girl was as freaky as they were told it would be. It was difficult to decipher when white men were interested in dating me because they were genuinely interested in getting to know me, or if they merely wanted to get a stamp on their sexual passport. Dating was near impossible, given that I have never been asked out by an Asian boy. Perhaps because I didn't exactly fit into any mother's ideal Korean girl, as I was very Americanized? I never knew. It wouldn't be until years later when I would tell my husband that, if I hadn't met him, I would've begun dating women. And I genuinely never knew if that made me bisexual, very open-minded, or that tired of being stereotyped as an Asian woman.

My attention then returned to Bennie's droning voice over the phone.

"Asians are really hot right now," Bennie continued. "We need more Asian girls in the club. You could make a lot of money."

"Right," I said, sitting with my complex feelings around Asian women who did choose to capitalize on the fetishes they were subjected to. If it's just going to happen anyway, why not make money off of it, right?

But did this mean these women were doing us a disservice by contributing to the fetishization and the stereotypes against Asian American women? Like May Wong, a hero in her own right, being the first Asian American woman to grace the silver screen . . . but at the same time, only able to play roles in which she was an "exotic" or "foreign" prostitute or spy, using her sexual prowess to take down the American government. Wong gave a big middle finger to Hollywood when she quit acting because she wasn't allowed to play other roles. She was very well aware. And I applauded her for her decision to refuse to play their game.

Hero? Or traitor? No. That would be too simple. Certainly, some of the Asian American women in Bennie's strip clubs were making fast money the best way they knew how because they were businesswomen. They knew there was good money to be made there.

The answer to my question of whether these women were taking these narratives back and empowering themselves ... the answer has to be "all of the above." Because any criticism of what they do is only a testament to the folly of the ones who believe in the stereotypes of freaky Asian women.

HEEM-PEH-RAH
(LET GO OF CONTROL)

The night I was leaving for basic training, I opened my computer to find an email from a name I had not seen in weeks. She had ghosted me up until the last possible minute—my best friend, allegedly.

> Joan,
> I know it's been a while. I've just been so busy. So much was going on, so I didn't have time to call you. Sorry I didn't return your phone calls. I just had a lot on my plate. I hope you understand.
> Love,
>
> Stacey

It was so . . . weak. An email? The cowardice of avoiding picking up the phone and calling me . . . the lack of apology for taking my money, the money I needed to get through my last month before leaving for the military. Yes, her brother had died, but my heart hardened. I felt that she was trying to use Peter's death as an excuse for her disappearance. I felt the opposite of sympathy; I felt emptiness. But I also felt indignant that she felt she could get away with treating me this way.

In that moment, I made a choice. I chose life. I chose the future. Instead of being stuck in the past with Stacey, I chose to open the next chapter in my life and start a new adventure in the military. Something in me had shifted: I learned something about myself. I had been reaching for the bottle to desperately regain control over my life, to pull away from my mother. In the chaos, I loved losing inhibition because it felt freeing from my mother. But I had completely lost control, and I didn't want to admit it.

Above all, seeing what Stacey had unraveled into made me see a version of myself that I didn't want to become. I never wanted my dependencies to get in the way of my relationships to the point where I would manipulate my friends to get what I wanted or needed. And I think I was loyal to a fault because all I had in this life were my girlfriends, since I had no real family behind me. So to betray a girlfriend, to me, was the most egregious of sins. And for the first time, I stood up to someone because they crossed a boundary of mine.

Stacey became a hypothesis for me: if I continued on this road, then I would become Stacey. I knew Stacey had loved ones to look out for her, to get her help. But for now, she was pulling everything in around her, like a black hole. I hovered my mouse over the email and clicked DELETE.

I wish I could say this was the point when I stopped drinking and that the frenzy to drink to forget would discontinue. However, the reality was I'd still have insatiable cravings—unable to stop after one drink. But this time, I knew I had to sever ties with people who would normalize it. From then on, I did successfully cut myself off from everyone from my old life. I knew I had a problem. I just wasn't ready to face it yet. But I knew one thing for certain: I finally admitted to myself that because I was trying so hard to maintain control, I had duped myself into believing that I was choosing to find myself week after week at the bottom of a bottle.

Before I left for basic training, I would tell my mother, in English, "I drank myself stupid because of you." Since my mother's English still wasn't very strong, confessing to her in English became a game—I was unsure of which parts she would understand, but I would lighten my load by telling her exactly how I felt. And this time, her only response was to reply in Korean, "How dare you blame that on me!"

APPA'S LETTERS

Shortly after I signed my Air Force contract, I found out that I was going to be a crew chief on the F-22A Raptor. It was the coolest job I could imagine for a female who was breaking stereotypes but a job that I truly felt underqualified for, given that I had no mechanical background. But since the Air Force sends crew chiefs to almost ten months of technical training after basic training and before landing at their home station, I told myself I had nothing to worry about. Like everything else, I would learn.

I once heard that a common response to getting off the bus to basic training was a "What have I signed up for?" kind of moment. But not for me. Sure, my stomach fell to the floor at times. And sometimes I could feel the tingle in my bladder, signaling that I was dangerously close to wetting my pants out of fear while having a drill sergeant's face two inches from my face screaming bloody murder at me. But regret? Not once.

Our bus pulled up to the barracks, which would be home for the next six weeks. It was so early in the morning, the sky was still dark. A drill sergeant trotted alongside the bus and pounded on the windows, screaming derogatory names at us; "turds" was my favorite.

Then the endless stream of commands poured forth and fell upon my ears. And from that point on, until I drove off that base, I hung on every single word and recited instructions over and over again in my mind to make sure I got it right, to avoid getting yelled at. I could not allow my auditory-processing issue to be a problem here. I would carefully place myself in the middle of any line, any group, to make sure I never went first for any type of activity, whether it be marching, getting our penicillin shots, or walking into the gas chambers to be tear-gassed. I watched the first trainees like a hawk. And whatever mistakes they made, I learned from quickly and would mentally repeat what I was expected to do. Not to say I never got my fair share of screaming from a drill sergeant. I would simply stare straight ahead and yell, "Yes, Sergeant!" And this part was important: don't make eye contact. Drill sergeants took it as a challenge. And lucky for me, being Korean American, this was something I was accustomed to, as my mother would frequently berate me as a child when I would look her square in the eyes while being disciplined.

After a couple weeks at basic training, we were allotted one phone call a week, like jail. That's what we were entitled to. I thought it was hilarious, because I was supposed to feel imprisoned, yet I felt free. And even the tempers of the drill sergeants felt like home, as the volatile temper of a Korean tiger mom was one and the same.

While we were standing in the outdoor courtyard, graced with a bit of downtime, we all waited our turn to make our phone calls on the pay phone. The sun was shining, and the Texas heat beat down on us. I welcomed it after spending the majority of my life in the dreary Pacific Northwest. As I stepped up to the phone, I felt nervous. Calling home meant acknowledging that the place was still there, waiting for me. That I could pretend to escape it, but had I really, if it still existed?

The phone rang an endless number of times. *Maybe she won't pick up*, I hoped. But abruptly, my mother's voice answered.

"*Yoh-boh-say-yoh?*"

I took a deep breath. "Umma . . . *nah-yah.*" *It's me.*

"Joan!" Then, as predicted . . . the yelling. "I open your mail! You owe Bank of America eight thousand dollars?"

And then, as predicted . . . the familiar anger, violation, and disbelief. But why disbelief? She had revealed herself to me multiple times. She knew no boundaries.

"What gives you the right to open my mail? That's illegal!" I said through gritted teeth. "How could you?"

"Joan! What did you spend money on? Credit cards need to be careful! So irresponsible!"

I was breathing hard. And, recognizing that for the first time I had control over the situation, I slammed the phone down.

Besides practicing drills, marching, and weapons training, and studying for a written exam about Air Force history and regulations, downtime in basic training was spent perfecting the folded clothes in our lockers, making sure our beds were made with tight hospital corners, and writing letters home. During my six weeks away at basic training, my father wrote me about thirty letters. The letters were almost always the same, typed on his beloved typewriter he bought from Goodwill:

June 6, 2010

Dear Sweety Joan,
How have you been?

Everything was difficult without you. Because you were not here anymore. You always brought many happiness to our family. Your mother and I waited for your phone call every weekend. We just wanted to hear your voice. Your mother told me you called here today. Thank you very much you called us. Are you everything OK or not? Are you learning about mechanical skills or maintenance skills? I was not very good in that fields. My younger brother who are living in NJ was very good and did better than I did because he was very sharp in that field and good hand skills. He used to own a printing shop in Downtown Seoul before he came to the US.

If I were you, I probably think of this way. I do not feel sad or I do not think I made a mistake to join to Air Force. I have already graduated 4 year university. I am better shape than other solders who still have to finish college. I almost finished 6 month's service already, therefore, I have to go another 5 and a half years to go. I can not get out right now anyway. I am learning new skills in free. If I go to Renton Technical College or Bellevue College, I have to pay at least 6 thousand dollars for two semesters. But I will learn these skills in free plus get pay my salary each month. About 5 and half years later, I can be discharge from Air Force. And then, I can enjoy all kinds of benefits which will be coming from US government. I can put in claims for benefits at United States government, State, County, and City governments when I will take tests (10 percent additional points). I can use GI scholarship bills for graduate school. Actually, my military life is strict but not too bad. I will enjoy my life in uniform.

You will have benefit from the US Veterans Hospital.

Who will take care your benefit? US VETERANS AFFAIRS?

NEWS:

1. COPPER RIVER KING SALMON AND COPPER RIVER SOCKEYE SALMON ARE HERE, SEATTLE. UWAJIMAYA GROCERY STORE COMPANY sold more than 500 pounds already. You see a piece of the Seattle Times, which shows a 30-pound Copper River King Salmon. That whole Copper River king salmon price is exactly $756.00. I saved some Copper River King Salmon fillet for you in our home freezer. When you come home, you can try it.

2. NEW KING COUNTY SALES TAX PROPOSAL HAS FAILED. Many King County employees will be lay off: police, fire fighters, and King County employees.

3. Many school districts continually laid off teachers. Seattle, Bellevue, Renton, and other school districts.

4. Ken Griffey Jr. had decided to retire immediately after the Mariners won against the New York Yankees at the Kingdom on 6-2-2010. He is 40 years old. He did not get the happy ending he deserved, but he brought joy to ball park and to the entire Northwest that will be remembered as long as baseball is played in Seattle. He retired after 22 seasons.

5. The Boeing Company and the City of Renton had a new agreement for leasing in the Renton Boeing field until 2050 (40 years). That is a good news for Renton Residents. Since the Boeing Dash 80 ushered in the dawn of the jet age in 1954, the world's best-selling commercial aircraft have been built in Renton. 42% of the jetliners in the air around the world today took their maiden flight from Renton Municipal Airport. With more than 6,300 delivered, a Renton-built Boeing 737 takes off or lands somewhere in the world every 2.3 seconds.

6. 2010 college graduates will not easy to find jobs.

7. Your mother worked 15 hours per week (three days per week).

Use 5 and half years to study. Time go fast. Look at me. I worked for QFC INC. more than 20 years Plus more than 20 years for UWAJIMAYA INC. I realy enjoyed two jobs over twenty years.

If you are busy, do not call us at weekend.
But you have to be safety. Try to find fun inside
of uniform. When you are difficult, talk to us. We
are your parents.
  We love you very much.
  Take care of yourself!
  God bless you!!
  Love, your mother and your dad

When my father's letters came, I would quickly skim
them. He would profess his love for me almost overabun-
dantly, in order to make up for the lack of affection I received
from my mother. He would remind me that they *both* loved
me very much. His words fell flat. But not because of what he
was writing; they fell flat because they fell upon my unfeeling
heart. I would fold his letters back up, almost dismissively. I
already knew everything that he wrote me; it was predictable.
I knew my father loved me very much. But after hearing it so
many times, it became white noise. And I had allowed it to
become white noise because these words did not come from
the one person I wanted to hear them from: I was indifferent
because he wasn't my mother.

ASIANS ARE PERFECTIONISTS

Basic training went by in a flash. Because, before I knew it, it was September 11, 2010. I arrived at my home base after being stationed at two training bases in Texas and another base in Florida for hands-on training, called "HOT" training. The first time I arrived in Anchorage, I found the wildness and openness astounding. Untamed greenery and vast mountains wrestled with the sky for space. At night, the temperatures dropped so suddenly, it hurt to inhale, but it forced me to feel alive. I visualized the lining of my lungs crystallizing with every breath. When I worked the graveyard shift on the flight line, I would stare upward, the Northern Lights teasing the skies feebly. It was so frigid, I could feel my vitreous fluid freezing over my eyes; it hurt to blink. One night, a fellow crew chief walked over to me on the flight line and caught me looking up at the sky. We could see a faint trace of green and blue.

"Aw, you can barely see 'em!" he exclaimed.

"Huh?" I asked dumbly.

"We're too close to the city lights. You gotta be farther out in the countryside, like Wasilla or something."

It didn't matter to me. His disappointment confused me, as it was one of the most beautiful things I'd ever seen. Me—a city girl who lived an enigmatic life, fiercely sheltered by her tiger mom but, contrarily, robbed of her adolescence and innocence too early to make sense of it.

My naivete confused many of the other Airmen. They all knew I had a college degree but had never seen someone who held such a childlike wonder at life. I barely knew how to cook for myself, I didn't know how to properly do a load of laundry . . . and I didn't know anything about owning a car, despite having one. I recall one day I came in for my shift, telling the other mechanics a light came on my dashboard. Loving a mechanical "challenge," they all began troubleshooting, asking me what the light looked like. I walked up to our office whiteboard and grabbed a marker. Much to their bemusement and slight horror, I drew a Check Engine light. When I saw the looks on their faces, I slowly put the marker down and knew I was supposed to feel embarrassed.

"How are you a crew chief?!" they demanded.

"We didn't go to tech school and learn about cars!" I shot back, defensively, feeling hot.

They shook their heads, and like most things, chalked it up to me "being a girl." I didn't do myself any favors.

One day, I was walking my friend's puppy, since we were on different shifts and the puppy had become destructive out of boredom. As I was walking down the street, a car screeched around the corner like a bat out of hell. A man was behind the wheel, and he rolled the window down.

"Run!" he yelled.

I froze.

"Moose!" He sped away without waiting for me to respond.

I stood there for a moment, and my curiosity got the best of me. I cautiously continued walking down the sidewalk and came to a stop once it was in my sights.

When I think of moose, I think of the children's book *If You Give a Moose a Muffin*. The first day I arrived in Anchorage, the other new arrivals and I were given a mandatory briefing on base. We were told two things: the first was that Anchorage has the highest rate of sexual assault against women, and the second was to stay away from the moose. During the briefing, I had mentioned feeding the moose, and the room went quiet. After all, I had fed deer, bunnies, and squirrels back home. The instructor looked at me and sternly said, "They're fucking dangerous. They're aggressive as hell, and they'll kill you if you get close enough. Stay away from the fucking moose."

"Yes, sir."

But I didn't think of the instructor's warning when I stood on the sidewalk. I watched as the moose, who, at eight feet tall, towered over a tree, munched on something as it tore off branches. Its legs were long and lanky—they looked awkwardly gangly, but I knew, based on what I had been told, not to be deceived by its appearance. I was accustomed to seeing deer in neighborhoods back in Washington. But deer ran away when you got too close. They were skittish. But the second the moose caught me in its sights, it locked eyes with mine.

Is this when I run? I wondered calmly. But the moose didn't mind me. Although it watched me with the puppy, who had become very still, the moose continued to chew. My eyes roved over its coloring: a muddy brown. Not a chocolate brown, like they're frequently depicted in the picture books. Its antlers were enormous and regally perched on its head, like a crown, creeping toward the sky like two corals. Satisfied, I slowly turned around and walked back to my friend's house.

I took a deep breath as I looked beyond the houses at the backdrop of the landscape. The sheer space in Alaska took my breath away. And I finally felt free of my mother, my past, and the future I thought I was damned to. I thought briefly of everyone I left behind. I stopped picking up phone calls if any numbers began with my area code. The limitless possibility of having full control over my being . . . I could cry with relief. Almost. Because by then, my heart had hardened. I hadn't cried since Stacey's brother's funeral many years earlier. And I didn't believe I was capable of crying any longer. Any tears I had shed before, in my previous life, had frozen over.

When I try to explain Alaska to people who have never been, I begin with talking about how close you feel to death. Every spring, when the ice would thaw, new bodies were found, mostly those of homeless people or others who had gotten lost in a snowstorm. Mother Nature is the epitome of raw, uninhibited power. And she'll fucking kill you if she wills it. While others recoiled, I delighted. What people didn't understand about me was how I loved being in a landscape that made me feel small and unimportant.

But the tragic thing about Alaska that I didn't understand then was that I should've been afraid. Because the thing I still couldn't escape was predatory men. As my first-day briefing reminded me, which I quickly forgot, I wasn't safe anywhere from the threat of men. Alaska, as it seemed, would also not let me forget it.

What was strange about being a woman in the military was that, despite being constantly exposed to sexual harassment, the comradery was inexplicable—my brothers in arms. The ones who were close to me were fiercely close to me and would defend my honor on my behalf when the others got out of line. I will never forget it.

There was one afternoon during turnover when an Airman demanded I get him something from the tool room. I refused. So he chucked a scribe at me. It flipped through the air but missed me by a mile. The guy standing next to me, Ruiz, who I adoringly called "Brother," jumped over the counter and started a fight. In my previous life, I lost a brother. But I gained many in the Air Force.

However, despite my brotherhood, danger still lurked, because I still liked to go out to the bars alone at night. I was a bit of a loner and had zero girlfriends. I wandered the bars in downtown Anchorage, meeting my guy friends and momentarily forgetting about the troubles of my past life.

"You know Butcher Baker?" my friend had eagerly asked me in a bar one night. "He's from here!" I vaguely remembered seeing books at the Base Exchange (or "BX," as we called it) checkout stand about the serial killer who had used his private plane to fly prostitutes into the mountains to murder them and bury their bodies. Eventually, the police found the trophies that he had collected from each woman, after one prostitute escaped and was able to identify him. During my time stationed in Anchorage, our streets downtown briefly shut down for the filming of *The Frozen Ground*, a movie about Butcher Baker, starring Nicolas Cage, John Cusack, and Vanessa Hudgens.

I wished it were the only period something sinister was poisoning the city. During my time stationed in Anchorage, notorious serial killer Israel Keyes would prey upon Samantha Koenig, our local coffee barista, in 2011. The coffee stand Samantha worked at was near our base, and my friends would visit it frequently. We couldn't believe it when her missing posters began circulating around Anchorage. While I worked the tool room, we would sit in the back office during turnover and listen to the radio. When country music wasn't blaring from the stereo—it was always country—the local radio DJs would relay Samantha's father's messages to the public, his pleas for her safe return.

The footage from the security cameras in her coffee stand would be released to the news outlets, and we would play them on repeat, hoping to see any clues or indication as to the identity of the abductor. The grainy video would show Keyes using a gun to force Samantha to walk off camera and across the parking lot, where we would later discover his truck was parked.

That winter I was driving onto base, listening to the radio as Samantha's father continued to beg for his daughter's life. Unbeknownst to any of us, her life had been extinguished, but only after Keyes had sexually assaulted her, then committed necrophilia on her frozen body, which he had stored in his shed. It was Christmas Eve. And little did I know, Samantha's father's exhausted, strained appeal would be the last time we would hear his voice on the radio.

I wish I could say the town was on edge—that I was unnerved a serial killer was hiding among us. But I was so desensitized, and living in a place where death surrounded us. I didn't know how to feel afraid of men anymore.

When credit card charges finally led police to close in on Keyes, he told them where to locate Samantha's body. He had finally dumped her body in a frozen lake before fleeing Alaska. Rumor had it he had been in Texas, using her credit card. I wish I could say I could finally breathe easy, but I knew that Keyes was not the only dangerous man left in Alaska.

BIG GIRLS DON'T CRY

t was October of 2010.

I had been carrying a weight on my chest for several months. But this time, it had become unbearable. The fluorescent lights were blinding me, and I was hyperventilating into a paper bag, sitting in a swivel chair in our aircraft hangar office. My supervisor, in his uniform, sat in front of me, trying to calm me down.

Sergeant Stanley was a balding man in his late thirties who reminded me of Jerry from *Parks and Rec*. He was kindhearted, and for that, easily dismissed at work; all kindhearted guys in the military were taken for granted, except by the few women who served. His forehead was wrinkled with worry, and his eyes darted between the office door and me. He held both his hands out, palms down, pushing down repeatedly on something invisible. He was stammering, and I could tell he was calculating what to do if I passed out on the floor.

They can't see me cry in uniform, I thought. *I worked too fucking hard to get here.* I was staring down at my sage-colored military-issue boots. My chest was tight, I couldn't breathe, and my vision was narrowing dangerously.

Sergeant Stanley tried to coach me. "Sung! Breathe!" Now he was looking panicked. "You're going to make yourself pass out!"

But I couldn't control it. I couldn't calm down. I felt like I was about to die.

Joining the military had done something unexpected. It gave me full independence, away from my mother, which was exactly what I had wanted. It had also done something strange to my alcohol dependency—I no longer felt the need to self-medicate or numb my feelings. Along with teaching independence, the Air Force drilled into us how to be type A: controlled, disciplined, perfect. I loved it. Because I got to control all of it. Room inspections, hospital-corner bedsheets that had to be folded as neat as a pin, scheduled exercise, clean and pressed uniforms—even hair had to be up to code. I thrived. But whenever there was a threat to my controlled habitat, I would crumble.

What sent me into a panic attack that day had occurred a few minutes prior. My new flight chief, Wildress, had stood in the doorway, looming as he always did.

"Sung, I need you to reorganize all the TOs."

"Why?" I asked, dismayed because I had organized them diligently according to number.

"I want you to organize them according to title. That's how we're supposed to do it."

"No, it's not . . ." I said slowly. He raised his eyebrows at my disobedience. "There's a TO that tells us how to organize it, and it's deliberately vague. It's a gray area. Which means it's our call, and there's nothing wrong with how I did it. I mean, I literally got the AMU Support Performer award after I organized the TO library. I know what I'm doing."

"Sung!" He raised his voice, exasperated. "Do as I say! It's an order. And you know what? I'm not dating, like you are, so I can work twelves until they're done. I have nothing waiting for me at home. I got all day." He smiled. But his smile made the hair on the back of my neck rise. It was the same smile the custodian had on his face the day I was assaulted. It was a lewd smile that acknowledged that I had no power, no control. And they would win.

He was disrupting my habitat, and I felt like I was losing control. Which meant, to me, nothing was in my control. I felt like I did when I lived with my mother. And when anything reminded me of my mother, my chest would constrict. I'd lose control of my breathing, and my stomach would churn.

The pressures of being in the military were immense. The intersectionality of being a woman of color in a predominantly white, male world; the crippling impostor syndrome; the inevitable sexual harassment; the rumors that I was sleeping with every man I spoke to . . .

When I arrived at my first home base, the guys started a bet to see who could be the first person to sleep with me. I was told that guys would talk about what they would do to my body if given the chance; one time a guy told his friends that when he masturbated, he fantasized about me. It wasn't long before his fantasy eventually got back to me. And I can't forget my favorite—the micromanaging. When a male coworker saw me working with a tool on the flight line, it was the same move every time: "Hey, can I see that for a second?" Then he'd take the tool away from me and finish the job himself. It was as if they couldn't stand watching passively as a woman did their job.

Another interesting phenomenon was that most of the men serving were from the South or from Texas. So they were inclined to offer to push my wheeled industrial-sized toolbox across the flight line for me because they wanted to be gentlemen. But I quickly learned that if any man saw me not pushing my own toolbox, I'd get grief for it and they'd whisper about me not pulling my weight. It was a trap—damned either way. Treat the woman like she's helpless, but then talk negatively about her if she accepts help. As a result, I never, ever asked for help—even when the sexual harassment got so bad that I spent every day after work crying in the shower. I got a tattoo on my rib cage that read in Latin, "Lord, give me strength," and whispered this to myself whenever I felt like the job was too much.

Even years later, when my husband would try to help carry in groceries or offer to hold my bag, I would still say brusquely, "Don't treat me like I'm helpless." It's still hard for me to ask for and accept help from a man.

Back in the hangar office, my supervisor was now imitating breathing exercises, as if I were in a birthing class. I clutched the paper bag around my mouth as I closed my eyes to stop the room from spinning. *Just don't let them see another woman cry*, I told myself. *I'll set us back fifteen years if they do.*

Later that winter, I was standing in the hangar when my supervisor jogged up to me.

"Sung, word is Thompson is out for Kadena. She is requesting you go in her place."

"What? Don't you guys leave in, like, a month?"

"Yup, you're going to have to get on top of your paperwork and make sure you're ready to go. We leave in January." It was December.

I was deflated. Part of the reason I joined the military was to travel for free. And I wanted to go to the depths of the earth, the farthest corner from where I grew up—the farthest point from my mother. But the one place I was not interested in visiting was Asia. I had no interest in Asia, where I thought I would feel the most displaced, despite being Asian. But it was my dual identity of being Asian American that made me feel like I had no business in Asia. A place where people would scrutinize me and expect me to naturally fit in, know the customs, or speak the language? It didn't matter that it was another country in Asia that was not Korea. No, no thanks. But I had no choice. Once it was decided I would take Thompson's place, I was thrust into briefings and had a checklist to work through to prepare for my departure.

The very next day, I was actively working on my temporary duty, or TDY, checklist. This included getting medical clearance (including immunizations), our TDY briefings, our bills set up for autopay, and a passport if necessary.

I was sitting at the computers in the hangar to make sure my paperwork was in order. The desks were all set up in a row, pushed to the back corner of the hangar. As I sat there, I could hear the conversations at the computers around me. Everyone was buzzing with excitement over the upcoming TDY.

One of the tech sergeants was on the other side, talking to the new Airmen about what Okinawa was like. He had been there several times before.

"You gotta go to the banana show! There's an old lady— God knows how old she is now—she's been there for *years*, and she'll shove a whole banana up her cooter and shoot out slices into the crowd. She would *cut the banana up with her vagina.* 'You wan' slice? You wan' slice?'" He would mimic her "Asian" accent.

As I peered through the gap between the computers, he was now standing over the young Airmen, jumping on one foot and pumping the other leg in the air as if shooting a gun. The boys were screaming in laughter and amazement.

"And the massage parlors . . . they're not *really* massage parlors. It's places where you can get 'happy-ending massages.' You feel?"

When he saw the boys' blank faces, he rolled his eyes.

"Hand jobs. You get hand jobs."

"Ohhhh . . ." the boys said in unison.

In retrospect, it's no wonder why everyone thought the Asian victims of the 2021 Atlanta spa shootings were prostitutes. There were two podcast episodes that profoundly informed my later understanding of what I was witnessing in that hangar: *Shoes Off: A Sexy Asians Podcast* ("Lisa Ling Wears Cargo Pants for a Reason") and *Archetypes* ("The Demystification of Dragon Lady with Margaret Cho & Lisa Ling"). Ever since *Full Metal Jacket*'s "Me love you long time," the association between Asian women and overt sexualization, fetishization, and prostitution was cemented for decades to come.

But why was Okinawa so sparkly? So enticing? These military men could find prostitutes in America. We lived in a country that was becoming more and more open with sexuality, and people were condemning the sex shaming of women. But when the older Airmen talked about Okinawa, the tone was different—because Asian women were freaky. We were seen by American society as being submissive. And this was the men's opportunity to take a peek behind the curtain and offer the women a chance at sexual liberation. Since Asian women were sexually repressed, these men would be the ones who would allow the women to be uninhibited, since the men were of a more sexually open culture—or so they thought.

Because Asian women are constantly subjugated to fetishization, Okinawa held a special place of interest for the United States military. And I wouldn't fully understand until my boots hit the ground in Kadena.

We left Elmendorf Air Force Base on January 13, 2011, at dusk, the day after my twenty-third birthday. We were set to leave on the twelfth, but they couldn't get the C-5 ready due to weather conditions, so we were grounded for another twenty-four hours. I celebrated my birthday alone in my dorm room, awaiting orders, with a pepperoni pizza.

The evening after, we all trudged across the flight line, the frost coating the cement runways, our foggy breaths slow and sleepy. We were all quiet, feeling the hangover from the depletion of adrenaline since we had been on standby for almost a day. I looked far out at the Alaska terrain, silently saying goodbye to the first real place I was able to call home. The sun tickled the tops of the forests and the obstructive mountains. I ducked my head as we all climbed the ladder to board our C-5. The next time our boots would hit ground, because of the time difference, we would miss a whole day—a jump into the future. And the next time we emerged from the C-5, we would be in the tropics.

Everyone warned me what it would be like to ride on a C-5: Badass. Boiling. Sweltering. Freezing.

It was all of the above.

I fell asleep quickly, maybe within twenty minutes of departure. This was partly because we were sitting backward and I had horrible motion sickness, so I knew it would be in my favor to sleep. But when I woke up, I was soaked in sweat. I felt like my uniform had become a weighted straitjacket. I felt an upcoming panic attack. Whenever I felt restricted, my anxiety would kick into gear. This time was no different. And the blistering heat felt as though we were in a boiler room.

I began breathing through my nose and listened to the conversations around me with great effort. The flight was so loud, much louder than a commercial flight, and it was roaring in my ear. The guys around me were shouting and laughing. It was no wonder I was jostled awake. We were all buckled in snuggly, our elbows almost tucked in for lack of space.

"Okinawans don't even want us there!" someone to my left shouted.

"Why not?" a voice shouted in reply.

"The fucking Marines!" Men nodded their heads in understanding.

I was missing something. I leaned in to hear more.

"They keep raping the fucking women!"

"I heard one of their guys stole a school bus!"

"Yeah, I heard that too!"

"Did you hear the one where a local woke up and a Marine was wasted and sleeping on their couch? They think they own the fucking place!" More outraged nods.

Honor among thieves.

Landing on the airfield in Kadena was a blur. It was late. I somehow found my ride to the base hotel—our temporary housing for the next three months. I had one roommate, another woman in the Weapons troop. One would think that women would grow a fast kinship in the military, where we were minorities. That wasn't the case. Women would look at each other critically, asking themselves one question and one question alone: *Are you going to set our gender back?* Each woman worked their ass off to hold their own, pull their own weight, and have a particular reputation (a hard worker who wasn't a "slut"). So, unless you were a nun, it was a hard game to win. It was competition, but you weren't really competing against each other; you were competing against the patriarchy that had pitted you against one another.

As I dumped my belongings and my military-issue green duffel bag on the hotel carpet, I breathed a sigh of relief that we had finally made it.

"I get the master. I'm higher ranking," my roommate said curtly. I didn't argue; I didn't even say a word. She retreated into the master bedroom. I opened the pullout couch. I plugged in my laptop and took a quick shower to wash the day off. I returned to my laptop to check my messages from friends and family on Google Chat, since it was the only way to reach me back then.

And then the messages came through.

Ding.

"You awake?"

Ding.

"Can we talk?"

Ding.

"Hey, there's something I've been wanting to tell you . . ."

Ding.

"Want to come over to my room?"

I was suddenly aware that I was getting more sexual attention than I ever had before from my married coworkers. And I knew why: because we were in Asia, I was no longer one of them. To my comrades, my fellow service members, I had become a plaything that was waiting to be unwrapped by a GI.

I closed my laptop and tried to sleep.

It was cherry blossom season in Okinawa. As the warm, gentle breezes rocked the trees, cascades of baby-pink petals floated down like a snow flurry—or if the wind caught them just right, like a curtain of lace. Since Okinawa was in a tropical climate, the heat was balmy, and the humidity clung to my skin like Saran Wrap.

But in contrast to Okinawa's beautiful pink bubble, all of us awoke to the disturbing news of the Tōhoku earthquake and tsunami, what would later be known as the Great East Japan Earthquake. It was 2011. A six-minute earthquake east of the Oshika Peninsula set off a tsunami, killing 18,500. To this day, there are still bodies unaccounted for. I watched the news that morning, seeing the gaping holes where earth and road once stood. My Facebook and Google Chat blew up, as friends and family members asked if I was okay.

But on the island of Okinawa, the air was calm. Everyone buzzed about the earthquake, checking on people they cared about, but once again, I was left pondering the uncertainty of life and death, feeling unperturbed.

On that lazy Saturday morning, I decided to run to the local BX to get a coffee. When I entered the sliding doors, I noted the red alarms mounted on the walls. When I first saw them inside Kadena's BX, I had asked a friend what they were for, since I had never seen them on our base in Elmendorf. He explained, "Well, keeping an eye on North Korea, for one. Why else do you think we're here?" And what was it that I felt? I prodded at the feeling: Guilt? Shame? Embarrassment at the distant association? I didn't tell a single soul my mother was technically a North Korean refugee, and I didn't mention it to my friend then. During the time we were TDY, which was part of a routine rotation, tensions were high (higher?) between North and South Korea. Military talks between the two countries had broken down, resulting in North Korea storming out of a humanitarian talk in February 2011.

On my way back from the BX to the hotel, I walked down a quiet road and stepped through puddles of petals. I noticed a familiar figure walking toward me on the same side of the street. I felt the flutter in my stomach as I recognized Ryan. But I wasn't wearing any makeup, so I avoided his gaze.

"Hi," he greeted me. "What are you up to today?"

"Coffee!" I laughed nervously, using the cup to shield my face. "Coffee run." I shrugged off my lame joke and continued walking, leaving him standing there, puzzled by my awkwardness.

During my time in Kadena, I started spending more and more time with Ryan's circle of friends, and therefore, more time with Ryan. And I was surprised at how quickly we became friends and how much of our conversations were filled with laughter and banter.

One evening, he was looking at me across a ridiculously oversized margarita on the table in our booth at a restaurant. We had finally agreed to go on a date, just one-on-one, to get to know each other better. I felt nervous and unsure. I could never distinguish when white men were interested in me just for sex, to fulfill some exotic sexual fantasy, or if they were genuinely interested in getting to know me better. But then again, before Ryan, I was never friends first with the men I dated. I always met them drunk, and I always kept them at arm's length. Whenever I felt true intimacy, I hid because I felt like there must be something wrong with them if they were genuinely interested in me.

Ryan was tall, six foot five, and husky. His dirty blond hair was buzzed, like the haircut all the military guys had, but he had a kind smile that always reached his blue eyes. He was from a rural part of Pennsylvania and was of German heritage (more specifically, Pennsylvania Dutch). It was refreshing that, for once, a date could tell me about his heritage rather than simply shrug and say he was "white," as if that were enough of an answer.

The restaurant lights dimmed; we had talked through the night.

I suddenly remembered earlier that day in the hangar, when the squadron was being briefed and the flight chiefs made the announcement.

"We just got word the Marines arrived this morning." The entire squadron had groaned in unison.

"You know what this means. Curfew is set to ten o'clock. Don't let any of us catch you off base after ten. If you run into any of them off base, don't start trouble. Most importantly . . . lay low."

So the Marines had arrived. I was bemused.

"If you get caught off base, just stay out all night," my friend whispered at my elbow. I nodded in understanding.

Back at the restaurant with Ryan, it was nearing that time. We had to get moving.

"It's closing time . . . Can I walk you home?" he asked. I felt a twinge of suspiciousness at his chivalry, but for some reason, the voices in my head that usually protest quieted, and I agreed.

We slowly walked back to the hotel and continued to talk. I was wearing a tank top and denim shorts, but the evening still held onto the heat of the day. And even if it were cold outside, I don't think I would have noticed. I felt safe with this man. I couldn't explain it. It was as if all these years, I'd been holding my breath around men, but around this man, I could finally exhale.

When our base lodging was finally within sight, I was simultaneously hoping he would ask to come to my room and hoping he wouldn't. He didn't know it, but he had already stepped into a lose-lose situation. But before I could read any potential signals he was sending about how this night would go, we both stopped in our tracks when we noticed a man sprawled on the walkway leading to the hotel. He had shaggy gray hair and wore jeans and a sweatshirt.

Ryan rushed over to him, knelt down, and began shaking and tapping his shoulders.

"Hey! Are you okay? Can you hear me?"

The man groaned in acknowledgment. I sighed in relief. I walked closer to where Ryan was crouched, and I immediately recognized the man was drunk.

"How did you get here?" Ryan asked. But the man was nearly incomprehensible and clearly blacked out. And it was obvious, because of his haircut and his facial hair, that he was one of the civilian contractors we deployed with, all of which would have been out of compliance if he was active-duty military. Not to mention, he wouldn't have had base access or been able to stay at the base hotel, which was conveniently located a sidewalk away.

"Sir!" Ryan was shaking him again. "How did you get here?"

"Coworkerssss . . . dropped me offff . . ." he mumbled.

Ryan frowned. "You went drinking with your coworkers? And they just dumped you here?" Ryan looked at me angrily. "That's fucked up!"

The man was already unconscious again. Without hesitating, Ryan grabbed his arm and hoisted it over his neck.

"Help me," he directed. Automatically, I stepped onto the man's opposite side and draped his other arm over my own neck. Together, we carried the contractor through the front doors of the hotel.

When we walked in, a woman stood with her head down at the front desk. When she heard the doors slide open, she saw us and her mouth fell open slightly.

"Oh my . . . what happened?" she exclaimed.

"Look," I said, "we don't know his name, but can you please give us his room number? We just found him outside lying on the ground." I had spent some time after college working at a hotel so I knew this went against hotel safety policies, but I prayed she wouldn't bring that up.

"Yes, yes, of course!" Her eyes never left the contractor. His head was hanging down, and his body was drooping heavily in our arms. "Oh, wait, but if we don't know his name, I can't give you the room number . . ."

I looked over at Ryan, raising my eyebrows as if saying, *What now?*

"I'll get his wallet. I'm sure he won't mind." Ryan shifted his weight and used his free hand to check the man's pockets. When he finally found a wallet, he tossed it on the counter. The woman picked it up and rifled through it until she found what she was looking for. She glanced at the ID, then turned to her computer to type in his name.

"Room 1106. Down the hall." She pointed behind the desk to her left.

"Is there any chance you could also make us a key?" I pleaded, hoping that she would indulge in one last favor, since I didn't see her pull a hotel key from his wallet when she looked for his ID.

"Yeah, sure." Without hesitating, she made us a key and slid it over the counter. With one hand, I grabbed the key, relieved. Ryan nodded, then retrieved the wallet off the counter.

"Thanks!"

We both slowly trudged down the hallway, which only seemed to get lengthier the longer we walked. At this point, I was soaked in sweat and hoped our date was over soon so I could take a shower.

My eye caught the door plaque: 1106.

"Here!" I grunted victoriously. Using the room key, I quickly swiped to open the door. "Get it!" I urged as the light blinked green. Ryan quickly reached out for the door handle, which, to our relief, opened immediately. We awkwardly shuffled the contractor inside, fighting against the weight of the heavy hotel door. Once we were in, I slapped the lights on.

Ryan ducked slightly, then boosted the man over his shoulder like a firefighter. He half threw the man onto the bed. I gave a long exhale, then cocked my head when Ryan walked over to the side of the bed to his nightstand. He proceeded to pick up the hotel pen and paper and jot something down.

When he caught my questioning eyes, he simply said, "Just in case he needs help, he can reach me tomorrow morning. I just want to make sure he's okay."

We left the room and made the long walk back to the elevator so I could go back to my floor and he could go back to his. But midway down the hall, I stopped in my tracks.

"Wait a second . . . the guy is blacked out. Don't you think he's going to freak out when he sees your name and number by his bed when he wakes up in the morning?" Ryan looked at me for a moment, and then we both laughed.

White men were hard for me to trust. But not Ryan.

I thought about the Tōhoku earthquake and tsunami and determined that life was short, but probably shorter for me, given my family's history of trauma and early death—strokes, for the most part. I scrounged around my memories and found one relative who died after a drunk-driving accident, because he drove himself into a ditch. Who knew how much longer I'd be on this earth?

As Ryan and I walked back down the hotel hallway, I looked at his face. In that moment, I took a deep breath and jumped in with both feet.

THE LOTUS FLOWER

It was the middle of March 2011, and we had returned from Okinawa on another C-5. Ryan and I had been seeing each other for three months.

When I returned home, I made the difficult choice to close an old chapter—an old boyfriend (if you could call it that). He wasn't happy to find that I had moved on and there was zero chance of getting back together. When I was in the Air Force, I only had two relationships: one with Ryan, and the first with a guy from the South. Because of my suspicion that every man was just trying to live out a sexual fantasy with me, I was curious about dating someone who appeared to be earnest, given his southern roots. But when I got close to Ryan in Japan, I immediately broke it off with the first guy. When I spoke to him, it was amicable; after all, it was nothing serious, and it was a brief season of casual dating. But several weeks later, unpredictably, he grew bitter and angry. I knew this because he began spreading rumors about me around our squadron, stories of fabricated sexual escapades, and calling me creative names like "whore" and "slut." It wouldn't be long before he would begin indulging the other Airmen with intimate details from our sexual escapades. But I noted that he conveniently excluded details of his impotence—our sex life had been almost nonexistent.

Nonetheless, his retaliatory behavior became more aggressive and quickly evolved into sexual harassment. He began calling me incessantly, leaving me messages on Google Chat and text, and yelling slurs at me as I walked into work.

I stood in the doorway of an office of four men, who were sitting in their chairs at their desks. They were higher ranking flight chiefs, the men we all reported to in the aircraft hangar. Everything in the office was beige. Beige walls, beige flooring, beige desks, beige cabinets . . . even beige faces. The men varied in age, midthirties to midforties. One was bald, and one had a scalp that was eagerly clutching onto the remainder of his youth. Another had a high and tight haircut you'd imagine on Dolph Lundgren. But regardless of their appearances, all of them in their Air Force uniforms, they all looked the same to me because they all wore the same expression on their faces. Because, in their eyes, I had given them the worst type of news.

I requested to submit an official complaint of sexual harassment. It was a flight chief's nightmare, because it was a bomb. No—it was a grenade, of which I had pulled the pin and handed it over to them. *What are you going to do with this now?*

The day I complained to the flight chiefs in their office about the sexual harassment, I watched them bounce my grenade around like a hot potato.

Dolph Lundgren warned me what a complaint like this would do to this young man's life.

"He's up for reenlistment, Sung. If you submit a complaint, he might not be able to reenlist. This will literally destroy his life."

I was enraged. "Sir . . . that's not on me. That's not my responsibility!"

"I know . . ." The flight chief appeared sympathetic. But for whom? I wasn't sure. "But think of the damage . . . I mean, are you sure it's sexual harassment?"

I shook my head in disbelief and glared at each of the men's faces. They were now nervously glancing at one another. I couldn't take another second. I stormed out of the office and into the hangar, with my head hanging in defeat. It was the custodian at the mall all over again.

Winter was coming to a close in Anchorage, Alaska, and the air was tinged with something sharp to the touch. The hangar doors were open, spilling the remaining daylight of the entire season onto the glossy but stained floor. The white surface didn't do much to hide streaks of amber grease and boot scuff marks. F-22As were neatly parked in the hangar, waiting for maintenance. Men hurriedly walked back and forth in their coveralls, all of them determined to make the jets "mission ready" before the end of their shift. Red "Remove Before Flight" streamers were fluttering in the breeze like ribbons, attached to the intake plugs on the jet. The oddly comforting smell of jet fuel hung in the air, hung on my clothes even, despite several washes.

What do I need to do to be taken seriously? I wondered, as I continued walking through the hangar, away from the flight chiefs' offices.

I heard the soft padding of boots hitting the hangar floor behind me. I turned around and one of the flight chiefs, Sergeant Johnson, was standing in front of me. He had dark hair and dark features, always had a chew in, and had a reputation for being stern and unsympathetic. Which was why I was surprised at what he said next.

"Sung," he called out, and caught up to me in the hangar. "Look . . . this is going to sound really shitty, but I'm going to give it to you straight." His voice was gentle but earnest. "I've seen this go badly for women. This is more than just ruining his life. I've seen Base Ops get involved in cases like these and twist things around. I've seen women get imprisoned for false claims because the men protect their own. You need to be careful. Now, I'm not telling you not to file a complaint, but you have to think about this, and I want you to know all the dangers of what you might do."

I stared at him long and hard. I didn't know who to believe, so I simply nodded my head and walked away to get back to work.

It wasn't until the following year, after I got out of the military, that I saw a news story go viral that was published in a prestigious magazine. An exposé of women who, sure enough, were imprisoned when they filed sexual harassment and assault claims in the military. Marines, Airmen, Seamen . . . women who were accused of fabricating stories of slander and lying under oath. And it wouldn't be until January 2022 that President Joseph Biden signed an executive order that would make sexual harassment an offense in the military's judicial code, the Uniform Code of Military Justice (UCMJ)—our law, our legal system. Women were allowed by President Harry S. Truman to join the military as of June 1948. This means that women were unprotected in our military for a whopping seventy-four years. A lifetime of rapes and harassment, reported and unreported.

Of course, the sergeant's warning that day in the hangar shouldn't have surprised me. I knew how the system worked. There was no human resource department in the military. I knew leadership ran on Good Ol' Boys clubs. I knew they would protect their own over a woman any day.

That day in the hangar, after I spoke to the flight chiefs, I walked from slot to slot. Each slot held one parked F-22A, and each slot had one toolbox belonging to a crew chief. Since the weather was warming but not entirely thawed, shrews were still fleeing from the fields into the slots for warmth. Mechanics liked to capture them, cruelly shove them into screw bags, then hang them on other Airmen's toolboxes as a prank. It had become my routine to walk the line and find them.

As I walked into an empty slot, waiting for its crew chief to finish turnover, I found a wriggling screw bag tied to the handle of a toolbox. I gently lifted the bag off the handle, untying the top strings that were also cinching the bag shut. I carefully walked out into the field beyond the flight line. It was bitterly cold, but I didn't care. I crouched amid the tall grass and loosened the bag. I gently tilted the opening, and one frantic brown shrew, no bigger than an apricot, thrust itself out of the bag, scurrying out into the field, thinking it was fleeing from its predator.

"Here, Sung. You got the Outstanding Performer of the Month award," Sergeant Wildress said apathetically as he thrust the bone-shaped wooden plaque into my hands. Our mascot was the bulldog, hence the bone. But this award looked like it was made with a leftover scrap of wood, and the bone was misshapen and rudimentary. And I knew what I was supposed to expect, since Ryan had the same award and it was perfectly sanded and sealed. I read the engraving on my award: *Joan Sung. 525 AMU. Outstanding Performer of the Month. August 2011.*

"Cool, thanks," I said, somewhat surprised. I thought everyone believed I was a drag, because of my label as a kiss-ass. "No ceremony?" I asked, joking.

He didn't respond. I could sense him mentally flipping me off.

Unlike most enlisted service members, I had a bachelor's degree when I joined the military. Everyone in my squadron knew I didn't belong there. And I was a pain in the ass, because I was always making suggestions to improve. And whenever I got an award, it was only because "I was a girl and a kiss-ass." It had stopped bothering me a long time ago.

It wasn't until I did some research when I got to my first home station that I found out I had been lied to. When an enlisted military recruiter gets a recruit without a college degree, that recruit goes in as enlisted (an entry-level workhorse until they work their way up the ranks). That enlisted recruiter then gets one recruit under their belt, as they are expected to meet a certain quota every month. A recruit with a college degree needs to join as an officer (an automatic leadership position) with a different recruiter. But given that I was in such a hurry and so painfully naive, I believed my enlisted military recruiter when she told me that my GPA was too low to be an officer—a lie so that she could keep me as a recruit and inflate her quota for the month. I found out months later that my GPA was actually high enough that I could have even been a pilot for the Air Force, if I had wanted. But instead, when my recruiter asked me what kind of job I wanted, I said, "Anything where I'm outside and working with my hands." And she smiled and responded with, "I have just the job for you." Just like that, I ended up being a mechanic on a fighter jet.

The rest of my time as an enlisted member was spent trying to go to Officer Training School (OTS). This can only happen by being an outstanding enlisted member with awards and a sterling reputation. By this time, I was volunteering for the base newspaper as a freelance journalist in my spare time and writing stories about the stellar work our Airmen were doing over at our squadron. The commander loved me because I was making him look good. And at this point, I had received multiple nominations and awards.

But the biggest reason why I was on leadership's radar was because of the work I had done while we were on TDY in Okinawa. I launched the Impact Initiative, where I organized three volunteer projects, each project increasing in impact from a micro to macro level. The first project was a baby-goods drive to help the NICU hospital on Okinawa. The idea was that our squadron would positively impact the base. Then I organized a squadron-wide beach cleanup to positively impact the environment. Lastly, I organized a World Vision fundraiser online to raise money, for a positive global impact.

When I returned from Japan, I came back with the reputation of a suck-up poster child, which I didn't mind, because I only had OTS in my sights. But then something unexpected happened. My flight chief, I discovered, was also interested in going to OTS. People started telling me that he thought I was a threat, because entry into OTS was highly competitive. I dismissed the rumors and focused on my own work.

It wasn't long before I got word that leadership wanted to put my name in for Senior Airman Below-The-Zone, an award that resulted in an early promotion to the next rank up. And the person who was supposed to put together my application package was my flight chief—the one who saw me as a rival. Despite the fact that this award didn't impact him whatsoever (he was too high-ranking for it to apply to him), there was an opportunity there regardless. I didn't get the award. A guy in the Weapons troop got it, and I heard he had used my Impact Initiative as his own example for his outstanding service to the Air Force, when he had only volunteered for the beach cleanup.

This incident forced me to recognize how I was treated in the military: like an unspoken hero whose back would be stepped on in order for men to advance in their careers, my hard work discounted and only seen behind the curtain. And it wasn't until about a year later, after that flight chief had left for OTS, that my new chief told me he looked at my application out of curiosity.

"You got hosed. Did you know that? He totally hosed you." Sergeant Murphy was grim.

But I was resolute. "It doesn't matter. I'm getting out when my time is up."

"Why?"

"Because I want to go somewhere I'm appreciated."

He laughed. "Sung, you're never going to get that any-where you work." And to a certain degree, he ended up being right. But in that moment, all I cared about was counting down the months until my contract was up with the Air Force.

It is not uncommon to see a lot of Asian Americans in middle management in corporate America, and not in high CEO roles. There's a YouTube video, uploaded by a chan-nel called Participant, titled "ASIAN: How You See Me." In this video, several speakers unpack the Asian American

Pacific Islander identity. But one man in particular refers to something called the Bamboo Ceiling. He explains that, "Oftentimes our culture, for instance, you know . . . my mom always tells me, 'Don't ask for a raise. Keep your head down. When you do your work, your boss will basically see that you're doing well, and he'll give you a raise.' But in America, it's not like that. In America, it's the squeakiest wheel gets the oil, right?"

Yes, *but*. Yes, but if you are an Asian American *woman* who is outspoken and assertive, you will never get that oil. Because we are bias disrupters, our intersectionality threatens the American understanding of what it means to be an Asian American woman, and in turn, it is more challenging for us to get that raise than if we were Asian American men.

BRINGING HOME A WHITE MAN

"Fuck!" Ryan yelled. "Fuck! It happened!"

"What? What's happening?" We were at his house, and he got off the phone with his supervisor.

"It happened. I got orders."

My stomach sank. "Where?" I knew I'd regret the answer.

"Aviano." Italy.

It was April 2011, and I still had two more years of my duty at Elmendorf. "What do we do?" I asked quietly.

We both fell silent for several moments. And finally, it was Ryan who timidly asked.

"Should we … get married?" Then he hurriedly explained, "If we get married, we can stop the orders. They'll try to keep us together at the same base."

I can't really explain it, but his suggestion didn't surprise me. We both felt at ease with each other, and it wasn't the honeymoon phase. He made me feel *safe*. And I had never felt so wholly safe in a relationship with a person before— least of all with a man.

"Let's look at rings," he suggested.

That very day, we drove to the Anchorage mall, and I picked the least expensive ring.

"Here, we'll leave it here, and I'll come back later and buy it and surprise you," he suggested.

I laughed at his effort to make it as romantic as possible despite the circumstances. I shrugged. "Okay."

Within two weeks, we had gotten engaged and asked our friend to officiate (in the state of Alaska, anyone can officiate) and invited two witnesses from our squadron to sign our marriage certificate. We eloped on a cliffside on May 14, 2011, somewhere in Alaska, where I refused to look down, because we were so incredibly close to the edge, we could've easily plummeted to our deaths.

The week after we eloped, Ryan received a call from our first shirt that it was decided we would both stay together in Alaska. We were relieved that we stopped Ryan's orders successfully.

"My mom will be heartbroken if she finds out I got married without her there," Ryan told me. Which left us with one alternative: to keep our marriage secret and announce to both our families that we only got engaged. I couldn't care less how my mother found out, but Ryan would do anything to avoid hurting his mother's feelings.

The month after we eloped, I flew home to lie to my mother in person that we were engaged.

I landed and made my way to baggage claim, then stepped outside as her car approached. My stomach fluttered. She stepped out of the car, and I just wanted to get it over with.

"Umma, look!" I held up my hand with the diamond ring. Her face grew dark.

"Get in car!" she barked at me.

I obeyed. During the car ride, I told her he was white. She was livid. But for once in my life, she didn't try to argue with me or try to control the inevitable. She knew that I was no longer under her roof and she had lost complete control. I somehow knew that she was angry because she wasn't involved in my decision, and I knew she would've preferred it if I married a nice Korean boy. We didn't say a word to each other the remainder of the car ride home. I thought about my aunt in Arizona who'd married a Black man and how much harder all of this must have been for her, so this should be a piece of cake—comparatively.

The following year was a grind. Ryan and I decided to go through a fake wedding ceremony, to give our families a chance to participate. Which meant I had to plan a wedding myself on a tight budget of $4,000. Because I didn't care about this ceremony, I randomly picked Pinterest boards to mimic. And because it was simple and inexpensive, I decided to replicate Jessica's wedding that I attended many years ago when her and Stacey's brother was still alive. I booked the same venue, not fully understanding how painful it would be to go back to a place I shared with the last person whom I truly trusted before Ryan came into my life.

The week before our fake wedding in Seattle, it was after dinner, about eight o'clock in Alaska, where we were stationed. Ryan and I were watching TV. My phone rang, and I saw it was my mother. It was later for her, so I knew something was wrong.

My mother's low, teary voice started, "Joan . . ." My heart slowed. "Jerry is dead."

Jerry was my cat. My beloved childhood cat of twelve years, and I hadn't seen him in years. I was just telling Ryan how excited I was for him to meet him. I began to sob.

"What happened?" I cried.

"He had tumor. He in so much pain . . ." Then she told me he'd been dead for a month.

"Wait . . . what?" I yelled. My mother told me that she wanted to delay my pain as long as possible but knew I would find out when I came home for the wedding and he wasn't there to greet me at her house.

"I didn't want you to be sad!"

I insisted this was much worse. Ryan was still sitting on the couch, trying to figure out what happened. He cocked his head and looked confused as he tried to understand the broken Korean coming from me while guessing at the responses from my mother on the phone.

"I want to protect you, Joan!" She, too, was crying.

I hung up.

"Ryan, my cat died a month ago!" I howled. I barely got out the words before I erupted into tears. Bewildered, Ryan awkwardly patted my shoulder.

I was furious at how my mother shared truths when she believed it was convenient for me. She had spent her entire life in silence, keeping things from me, thinking she was protecting me. Our family secrets were my dead cat. Only when she believed I was truly ready for something would she reveal it. But what she didn't understand was that it was the holding back that was hurtful. Her secret keeping absolved me of any guilt from keeping secrets from her, which is why I never told her about my elopement or any other details about my personal life, including my multiple assaults.

After a year of wedding planning, the big day had finally arrived. It was June 10, 2012. We didn't schedule the ceremony for the same day as our elopement, because we discovered later it was actually less expensive to book a venue for a weekday than a weekend. So we picked a random weekday and paid our $300 deposit. I was sitting in my wedding dress at the head table at what I called the dog and pony show. It was June, and the weather perfectly replicated that day I watched Jessica walk down the aisle with her brother in his wheelchair—that carefree day she swung her bouquet by her side, so casually that it made me laugh. Why my subconscious thought an easy wedding plan would trump any residual feelings of nostalgia, pain, and disappointment, I would never really know.

It had been a year since Ryan and I eloped on the cliffside in Alaska. But because we were committed to not devastating his mother, here we were: an entire ceremony put on for someone else's happiness, despite the fact that I was supposed to be the bride. Nonetheless, I was still enjoying myself, as it was an opportunity to spend time with some of my childhood friends. Ryan approached the table and sat next to me, both of us watching the crowd of people socializing.

"Have you ever noticed that your mom never lets your dad talk?" Ryan asked.

I scrolled through my memory. I knew, but I had never put it into words. My mother was always interrupting my father's stories to tell him that he was rambling, or speaking nonsense. This had been going on my entire life, but I never once analyzed it.

"Also," Ryan continued, "about what I said about being worried that my nana would be upset I'm marrying an Asian girl . . . I'm sorry. I'm an idiot. I talked to my mom about it, and she reminded me that Nana has an adopted grandson from Korea—Derek. He was adopted when he was a baby."

"Really? You have someone Korean in your family? That's crazy!" I was surprised that he had never mentioned Derek before.

"Yeah . . . for some reason, I just don't think of him as Korean? If that makes any sense?" Ryan shook his head, as if trying to figure it out himself.

What I thought was funny was that Ryan was trying hard to reassure me that his family didn't have an issue with me. But it didn't even occur to me that I would be the one who could potentially be rejected from a family, when I was worried about my own family's ability to accept Ryan as a white boy. Fortunately, though, when my mother met Ryan, she fell in love with him immediately. This polite small-town boy was a perfect substitute for a nice, quiet Korean boy.

As Ryan and I sat at the head table, my thoughts drifted to Derek. He was adopted as a baby and raised by a conservative white family in rural Pennsylvania, who raised him entirely as their own, in their own culture. I wondered: *What would it be like to be Asian American but be culturally white? What would it be like to not feel any real connection to your heritage in a society that will only define you based on how you look?* Then I realized that I had spent my life having people impose their expectations on me based on how I looked. How society had constantly told me what it meant to be Asian American, but I was never able to define it myself. How my Korean culture and my Korean family told me I was supposed to be one way, but my American culture told me I was supposed to be something else; I was caught in between. I belonged nowhere.

My eyes wandered to my father, smiling happily by himself. My mother stood behind him, chatting with guests. *Maybe Derek and I have a lot in common*, I thought.

A few months after our wedding, when we were back at our duty station in Alaska, Ryan came home distressed.

"You'll never believe this," he said. "I was given a chance to work on a project on the F-22, and I was denied top-secret security clearance. Do you wanna know why?"

"What? Why?" I asked incredulously, since Ryan was known for being a model Airman at our squadron.

"Because you're Korean, and your parents are immigrants from Korea. It's because they're scared someone in your family might have North Korean ties."

"What, like a spy?" I laughed dryly.

"I don't know."

I felt guilty that my heritage had robbed my husband at a once-in-a-lifetime chance. But most of all, I felt perplexed, because my mother's side *is* North Korean. But that was before the Communist takeover. *Didn't they understand Korean history? Don't they understand how many of us actually have North Korean blood? What are they so afraid of? That Communism is tied to heritage?* It was a question that would never be answered. But the answer I did receive was to a different question: why so many years ago, a federal agent from DC was sent to interview me when I had joined the Air Force. Although he never asked me outright if I had North Korean ties, there was something off about that interview. It wasn't standard to be interviewed. And I actually didn't have a criminal record. In that moment, what made the most sense was that the agent wanted to assess what kind of American I was. Because if I were in his shoes, I would guess the most threatening thing about me wasn't that I was busted at a party and temporarily detained by the police. It was my heritage.

The questioning reminded me of the No-No Boys of World War II—the Japanese Americans who refused to swear loyalty to America on principle, and were interned or incarcerated as a result. Would I ever have been so admirably defiant? Many nisei (second-generation Japanese Americans) joined the US military to fight against Japan after Pearl Harbor and after the incarceration of the Japanese Americans, as a response to Executive Order 9066. Many wanted to prove their loyalty to the country. Many of them saw fighting for America as the only way to get their family out of the incarceration camps. There were some among the Japanese American community who did not understand how these young men could fight for a country, fight against what some of them felt was their true homeland, when this very country was responsible for such vile discrimination. My own independent study into the sentiments and motivations of the issei and nisei led me to determine that it's way too complex of an issue to really categorize.

Because when I think about George Takei's TED Talk, "Why I Love a Country That Once Betrayed Me," one thing is clear . . . this country will always represent hope for many. This country will always represent possibility for the future, as long as there are good people who are fighting to be heard.

ONLY WHITES ALLOWED

About a month after Ryan and I had our ceremony, we were happily situated back in Alaska. Summer had arrived. I moved out of the base dorms into Ryan's house in Anchorage, which we shared with six other roommates. To describe it as chaos would be an understatement—it was a glorified frat house. Being crammed into a small, two-story house meant hearing all of the fights between girlfriends, all of the makeup sex. I came home one day after one of the guys' girlfriends had a whim to spray-paint their TV blue, in the bedroom. The door and windows were closed, and it wasn't until she emerged from the bedroom that we knew the source of the fumes. Her pupils were dilated, and she quickly apologized before whipping out a can of Febreze and walking down the hallway, depleting the entire can into the air. Ryan and I coughed and sputtered, wondering if we were also high and hallucinating, while simultaneously hoping we didn't get lung cancer.

A door down the hallway opened, and our friend peered out.

"What is happening?" Boseman cried, barely getting out the words before coughing.

"Don't ask!" I managed, before waving him back into his room.

Ryan wanted to spend the next weekend bike riding, so Boseman and I went without him on a day trip to Alyeska for their blueberry festival. Boseman was one of the first friends I made when I arrived at Elmendorf. He was half Japanese and half Guatemalan. He had a blinding smile, which revealed a mouthful of what I used to call "perfect Chiclets," just to tease him.

After a morning of perusing blueberry jams and blueberry-themed decor, we headed home. When we realized we were hungry, we stopped at one of the few restaurants we saw on our drive, which happened to be in the middle of nowhere.

We saw the letters "BBQ" and eagerly walked through the front door, our stomachs growling and protesting our neglect. The chatter stopped as people turned around in their chairs to look at us. A waiter hurried up to us.

"Sorry, we're closed," he said curtly. I looked disbelievingly around the room where plenty of people were eating. The smell of smoked meats hung heavily in the air.

"What do you mean?" my friend asked.

"We've sold out of barbecue for today."

"How do you sell out of barbecue?" I asked, unconvinced.

"Look, we don't want any trouble." The man turned and walked away. The patrons continued to chatter to one another as their orders were being brought to their tables.

We slowly walked outside, back into the warm summer air that was only a guest in Alaska. I looked at my friend. He looked at me.

"Was that what I think it was?" I asked him.

"I think so," he said slowly.

We never spoke of it again.

Back then, I thought that it was easier to ignore something that causes you grief rather than face it head-on. Today, I'm not so sure I feel the same.

GENERATIONAL TRAUMA

That fall, snow began to appear on the ground to make way for the new season. Ryan and I decided to move out of the house and into our own apartment in Eagle River, Alaska, a sleepy town outside of the bustling city of Anchorage.

One Saturday afternoon, we got up early to drive to the local coffee stand that served coffee out of a red caboose. And we drove past the same dead tree we did every weekend. But this time, I gasped as I caught a glimpse of the tree. It was filled with about fifteen bald eagles. Ryan instinctively pulled off the side of the road, and we both fell silent and stared. Yet again, Alaska managed to remind me of her wild beauty. The gnarled tree had thick branches that threatened to tear a hole in the sky. It was almost bizarre; I had never seen anything like it, and I sat there confused, as I thought eagles were normally solitary creatures. But they had found each other that afternoon. Not in the wild but in a quiet town, home to native Alaskans who were accustomed to these reminders of nature. Quite a few of the bald eagles turned their heads to scrutinize us with one shrewd eye. Some tilted their beaks toward the sky, as if they were turning a nose up at us, like we were beneath them. And we were. After all, Ryan and I were the guests in Alaska. We could never claim that land to be our own.

I wondered then if a dead tree full of bald eagles was an omen. And if it was, I wondered what it meant.

That same afternoon, I was watching a KFC commercial on our couch in the living room. Ryan had dropped me off at the apartment because I wasn't feeling well. He was off running errands and picking up groceries for dinner that night.

KFC always reminded me of my childhood; it was a treat whenever our parents had the money to spoil my brother and me. Usually, seeing the golden crispy skin of fried chicken would have my mouth watering. But this time, I sat up with a jolt. A wave of nausea hit me, and I covered my mouth with one hand while using the other to push myself off the couch. I bolted into the bathroom and made it just in time to vomit into the toilet. As I panted hard, my breath suddenly caught in my throat as comprehension set in. I couldn't remember the last time I had my period. Still on my knees, I clambered over to the sink and began pawing at the bottles of cleaner and boxes of tampons until I found what I was looking for.

Ryan and I had a pregnancy test under the sink for when we were ready, but we weren't planning on having a baby anytime soon. But I didn't hesitate to hop onto the toilet to take the test.

By the time I managed to zip my pants closed, the two bright pink lines had appeared on the stick: pregnant. But instead of being excited, the first thought to hit me was, *Am I also going to hit my child? Is that something that one can control? Or is it like a genetic thing that gets passed on from parent to child?*

I slumped down on the bathroom floor, still clutching the pregnancy test. My eyes fell upon the vent that was perpendicular to the linoleum, a few inches from the ground. I noticed that a spider had spun a clumsy web over the slots of the vent. I watched as the air kicked on, and she struggled as her web trembled threateningly. I felt sorry for her. The spider, which had a speckled brown-and-white pattern on its distended belly, quickly began spinning more web once the air turned off. I watched as she attempted to make repairs, and fight against something inevitably set to destroy it. I briefly considered getting a jar and putting her outside. But it wasn't until I saw a white speck toward the bottom of the web when I realized what was actually happening: the spider wasn't spinning to repair her web. As if on cue, she scurried down and grabbed the white bundle—her victim, probably a gnat that took a wrong turn, that would now be her lunch.

"Fucker," I muttered as I watched the spider creep victoriously back up the web, where it perched and feasted. I had forgotten that the creature I had taken pity on was a predator who refused mercy to her prey. But you can't get mad at a spider for doing what a spider does; it's in her nature.

In that moment, I promised myself that I would do everything in my power to be the opposite of my mother— to fight against my nature. Every decision I would make as a mother I would have to make twice: once as myself, and once as my mother, to ensure they were not aligned. I looked down at my belly. *You and I are going to talk our conflict through. You might hate me at times, but not for the reasons I hated my mother.*

After my pregnancy test, I made an appointment at the base hospital with the ob-gyn the week after next. When the day of my appointment finally arrived, I checked in and sat down in the waiting room. A woman across the way was beaming at me. I tried to avoid eye contact and turned my body away from her in my chair, as if to nonverbally communicate to her that I wasn't interested in small talk. But ignoring my signs, she stood up from her chair, walked over to me, and plopped down in the chair next to me. I looked at her, offended at her optimism.

"Hi. How far along are you?"

"I'm in my first trimester," I responded curtly, trying to discourage conversation.

"Isn't it so exciting?" she asked dreamily.

"Is it?" I was unsure. I was still incredibly nervous about becoming a mother and hurting my child.

"I thought I had a miscarriage," she said. I suddenly felt guilty for my feelings. "But then we found out the hospital got the test results wrong!"

"How . . . ?"

"Well . . ." she said, leaning in. She was bubbling over. "They accidentally switched the vials from our blood test. The results we got were for someone else!"

My eyes widened at her, horrified. "That would mean . . ."

"Yeah, they had to call some poor girl and tell her that what they thought was her healthy baby had died. Can you imagine my surprise, though? I had already called my husband on a video call and told him that I lost the baby. He was in Afghanistan. That was hard . . ." Her voice grew heavy. But all I could think about was the other woman.

How would it feel to have lost your baby? Would I be sad, given that I wasn't even sure I could be a good mother? I poked at my feelings. My feelings gave me nothing back. *How much choice do you have to be the mother you want to be? Are my fears legitimate?*

My attention returned to the woman glowing in her seat, looking lovingly at her belly.

"I'm really happy for you," I offered.

"Thanks!" she said cheerfully, patting her bump.

I stared at her, hoping that my feelings of excitement would soon arise too.

ASIAN WOMEN ARE SUBMISSIVE

That Monday, I found myself back at work in the hangar. Ryan and I planned to keep our baby news to ourselves—or so we thought.

In the hangar office, my new flight chief, Sergeant Wildress, was staring at me and grinning lewdly. That smirk he gave me whenever I disagreed with him almost said, *We'll see about that* . . . And it would send chills down my spine. He looked at me as a rancher would look upon a wild horse that needed to be broken. And he was up for the challenge.

"Sung, you're volunteering this weekend for Airmen Against Drunk Driving," he jeered. He was fully aware his rank gave him liberty to give me orders I had to follow, unless I wanted a Letter of Reprimand, a mark on my record.

My eyebrows shot up into my hairline. Airmen Against Drunk Driving was a base program in which sober drivers drove drunk Airmen home after picking them up from the bars. Females who were assigned to duty were equally as responsible for driving around town and collecting drunk men in their cars.

"Uh, no, sir. I'm not."

There was that look again. That look made me sick to my stomach, as I found it utterly humiliating and patronizing.

"Yes, you are. You are being volun-told." He turned around to walk away.

I knew what he was doing. He expended his energy making my life a living hell, giving me additional duties to do, while the men were spared. I was treated no differently than a Greek Row freshman going through a hazing process.

"Report me," I dared.

He slowly turned around.

"You heard me right. Report me. I'm in my first trimester, and I am not driving to the bars to be alone with drunk Airmen in my car. And if you tell me I have to, I will go straight to the first shirt about how you are jeopardizing my baby."

"You're pregnant?" His eyebrows raised ever so slightly over his mildly interested expression. He rolled his eyes and threw up his hands. "Fine," he spat. And as he turned, he muttered, "Brat."

As I stood my ground, I wondered where my assertiveness had come from. But I know now: it was my mother who had taught me to be defiant, because she was the first person I learned to rebel against. I knew that now I had a chance to be brave for someone other than myself. Being Korean, I initially felt at home in the military, where we were expected to respect rank, similar to Korean culture, in which we were expected to respect our elders. But this time, I drew a line in the sand, and I knew that defiance has a time and a place. Defiance is a gift. And I can genuinely thank my mother for that.

My time in the military would eventually come to an end. As I reflected on my time so far in active duty, I realized that it was challenging because I was a woman, but for the most part, my loud mouth was actually appreciated among men.

The fact that I was a strong woman impressed them, because my strength reflected well on the uniform and I didn't make them look bad in an environment where hypermasculinity was valued. But once I entered the civilian world, my time in the workplace became challenging. Because everyone, men and women alike, would have been more comfortable with me fulfilling the stereotype of the submissive Asian American woman—as that was more predictable.

DOUBLE CONSCIOUSNESS

Fall finally succumbed to winter, and winter announced its arrival loudly and briskly. In Alaska, summer and winter were the most prominent of seasons, and the most memorable. Winter would hold its icy grip, refusing to release, and just as tenaciously fight for its chance to unseat fall. By October, there would already be substantial snow on the ground. Ryan and I used the snow on the porch as our beer cooler. We nestled our cans and bottles outside so we could make space in the fridge.

But that November, we sought respite from the snow. Ryan and I took leave to Honolulu for his twenty-fourth birthday. We flew out November 10, 2012. We were sitting on a tour bus, and my stomach was rolling away on the floor as we flew over the bumps on the road, all of us rattling around like dice in a game of Yahtzee. Palm trees whizzed by the window as island music played on the radio. But it didn't matter. The only thing I could think about was *The Baby-Sitters Club*—the series of young adult novels that I loved as a child. I was in my twenties now, but I could remember the plot of one book as though I had read it yesterday. It was the one about Claudia, the Japanese American character, and her trip to Pearl Harbor—the very destination I was headed to on this bus.

When I was in fourth grade, I read about Claudia visiting Pearl Harbor. She was terrified that she would be subject to a racially motivated comment wrongfully blaming her for what happened in Honolulu, Hawaii, in 1941. As I sat on the bus that day, I felt the same fear.

Because here I was, on a bus to Pearl Harbor, just as Claudia was. But why would I be afraid if I was not Japanese? *Well, because no one can tell the difference*, I thought. Instead, I sat on the bus, tense, as though waiting for someone to strike at me. My eyes scanned the bus and immediately saw the elderly man sitting directly across the aisle. He wore a navy-blue flight cap donned with military pins. He clutched a cane and muttered angrily to himself. The blonde woman sitting next to him, perhaps his daughter, was reassuring him quietly and rubbing his arm. My stomach clutched—a veteran. And based on his age, a World War II veteran. I stared at him. I caught his eye, and he glared at me. I quickly looked away.

For the remainder of the ride, I saw him huff and shake his head. *At me? Oh my God, he's going to call me a Jap.* I looked at his cane again. *What do you do if someone smacks you with a cane? Is it like being attacked by a bear? Do you curl up into a ball and protect your head? Oh, wait . . . oh, shit, with a bear you're supposed to get really tall and make loud noises . . . Hell, that might work.* The veteran was sighing audibly.

"Ladies and gentlemen, we are getting close to Pearl Harbor," the driver announced on the intercom. The veteran groaned. I looked at him like he was a Hot Pocket ready to explode in the microwave. He fiercely whispered something to his daughter. She looked worried. We made eye contact. *Were they talking about me?* I looked away, pretending not to stare. He began impatiently thumping his cane on the floor of the bus as if extinguishing the life of invisible bugs. A few more minutes trickled by. I wiped the sweat off my forehead with my clammy hands. I desperately glanced at the veteran once more. *Get really tall and make loud noises*, I reminded myself.

"We have arrived!" the driver informed us cheerfully as we pulled into the parking lot. The veteran finally smacked the seat in front of him with his palm. I balled my hands into fists. *I will yell at a war hero if I have to!*

"Finally!" the veteran roared. "Don't you know the new iPad comes out today?" he shouted at the driver. His daughter covered her face with her hands. It was as if someone popped the cork off the bus, and the air began to release. The tourists on the bus slowly pivoted in their seats to stare incredulously at the World War II veteran, donning a flight cap and military pins, who cared more about getting his new iPad than revisiting Pearl Harbor.

I let out an awkward laugh. No one minded me.

Before our flight out from Honolulu to go back home, we stopped at Walmart to grab flashlights to check out some lava tubes on Hilo, the part of Hawaii where there were generally fewer tourists, due to its cooler temperatures. It was our last day in Hawaii. Ryan was waiting for me in the car, and here I was in aisle 13A, pondering over a variety of flashlights.

"Hey! You gettin' reddy for da hurricane?" An employee stood at the end of the aisle, calling down to me. Puzzled, I looked around to see who he might be talking to. I was the only one in the aisle, clutching three flashlights. He mistook me for a local. I grinned, taking it as a compliment as I called back to him, telling him I was only visiting. He smiled, made a *shaka* gesture with his hand, and walked away.

As I walked with my items to the checkout, I realized sadly how much I would miss Hawaii: in a country where I am constantly reminded of my otherness and being asked, "Where are you from?" Hawaii is the only place where people assume I belong.

TWO IS TOO MANY

In retrospect, the remainder of my time in the Air Force went by quickly. When I reflected on my experiences, I'd feel nostalgia and a tinge of regret I didn't stay a bit longer. And I was forever grateful for the independence the Air Force taught me. But above all, I knew I made the right call: the one thing I needed to escape was my sexist pig of a flight chief, Wildress. There would never be another person who made my gut so uneasy, who made my chest constrict. And I'll never quite be able to put my finger on it. I chalk it up to my women's instinct that, out of survival, I had to get away. Ironically, I had joined the military to escape my mother. Now, I just needed to get out to escape another controlling person who had a dangerous amount of power over my life and couldn't be trusted with it.

During my last winter as active duty, I successfully processed my paperwork to get out of the military. I was lucky that I had no employment gap, as a fellow Air Force wife quickly got me a job for Xerox. It was an office job, where I would be a database analyst until it was time for Ryan's time in the Air Force to end. He had about two years left, so it was simply a waiting game for me. I had just started my second trimester of pregnancy.

I read in a baby book that when a pregnant mother is distressed, the body releases cortisol to the baby, and the baby also feels the effects of heightened cortisol, resulting in a tense and stressed-out baby. This was my worst fear, as I couldn't imagine a baby having my level of anxiety. So I stressed while I worried about being stressed.

Ryan and I didn't even have a chance to consider baby names before my mother called me. She insisted that I oblige in a Korean custom where the baby's grandfather chooses the name of the baby. After a list of names I hated, like Gunner and Canon, I began feeling angry at my mother for, once again, taking control of something that should've been exclusively mine.

Ryan's father finally landed on the name Gabriel. It was the name he and his wife had reserved for their own baby, Ryan's half sister, when they thought she was a boy. Loving the whimsy of this story, I seized the name as quickly as possible and thanked him before he could change his mind.

But then I started getting missed calls from my father while I was at work. He would leave voice messages, expressing concern about the biblical implications of Gabriel. Then my mother's missed calls and voice messages began coming in, telling me to ignore my father.

The entire situation made me exhausted, because it was so typical of my mother to try to control everything in my life and to create chaos along the way. If we could have had a secret baby, I would've chosen to do so.

My phone rang again, but this time, I was able to pick up. My mother reiterated everything in her voicemail, demanding I ignore my father and his concerns. I mindlessly agreed.

"And, Joan, I thinking a lot . . . only have one baby. Because two is too many and too hard." I chose to ignore the fact that I was the second of her children.

On April 20, 2013, Gabriel was born, weighing a whopping ten pounds. Ryan was six foot five and I was five-five with narrow hips, so the labor was intense and challenging—especially because my mother didn't tell me anything about childbirth. No warnings, no advice . . . it appeared that childbirth would be categorized with sex and periods: off-limits for discussion between a mother and daughter.

When I was able to hold my newborn, I could only think of his future birthdays. My mind was flooded with memories of how, on the mornings of my birthday, my mother would tell me that I needed to celebrate her instead, and how it wasn't my day. It was hers, and I should tell her "thank you" on my birthdays. She would tell me how I caused her so much pain in labor, and how birthdays should be more about what mothers went through.

"I promise, I will let you have your birthdays," I whispered to my sleeping newborn. "I won't hijack your day, and you won't owe me anything."

CHRIS HAS A DAUGHTER?

When Gabriel turned nine months old in 2014, Ryan's contract was up. Because he still wanted to work in aerospace maintenance, Boeing made the most sense. We decided to settle in Seattle, my hometown. I had mixed feelings about moving back to where my mother lived. I was deeply anxious about her living so close—too close.

Soon after we moved all our belongings back to Seattle, we visited my parents' house. I was sitting cross-legged in the living room of my childhood home. Ryan was at work. I looked around, feeling surprised that, despite moving back, I no longer felt anchored there by my mother.

My dad was also sitting on the floor, across from me, beaming. It was traditional for a Korean family to sit on the floor this way. My mother was bustling around in the kitchen, making me something to eat.

"Joan is number one!" he said to me, giving me a thumbs-up. I laughed. His English is much better than my mother's, as he had been working at that grocery store for over twenty years, while my mother was mostly involved in our Korean church. "*Wuahh...*" my dad said, impressed. "My daughter is so tough, in the Army!"

"I'm not in the Army, Appa," I said for the millionth time. "I'm in the Air Force."

"When I was in the Korean Army, like you, one time I show up to my commander. I was so drunk! Like this!" He saluted, waving his body back and forth. "Ha!"

I smiled. I rarely got to hear his stories about when he was younger. When he did get a chance to share his stories, there was always a colorful element he added, an element of playfulness, as if he molded his stories to the amusement of his audience.

My father continued. "I said, 'Sir, I don't want to go to war. I'm almost done with my two years.' In Korea, you only serve for the two years." He held up two calloused, crooked fingers, evidence of his hard work and labor over the past few decades.

"And then what?" I prompted him.

"And then he say, 'Okay. You don't gotta go to war. You can go home.'"

"Really? Just like that?" I said, amused and half believing him.

"Just like that. That's how I missed fighting in war."

"Hm," I said easily, unsure of which war he was referring to but not wanting to interrupt him.

My mother walked into the living room where we were sitting. "*Yohboh! Gimanheh!*"

Obediently, my father clammed up. I didn't think twice about it. She hated his rambling. It was moments like these I wondered why they didn't just divorce. It was as if she couldn't stand the sound of his voice. But I looked at my father's face, lined and etched with memories and laugh lines. His face looked content. But I felt sorry for him.

"Joan." My mother was now bringing in plates of *kimchi* and *keembop* for us to eat. She placed them on a small wooden table that stood no more than a foot off the ground. "Did you gain weight?" she asked in Korean. I rolled my eyes. Other times when I come over, she says I don't eat enough. I can't win. "Chris coming home soon. He bringing his *ddal*." She looked determinedly at the plates she was serving, and her mouth was in a straight line. *Wait. Did I hear that right? His daughter?*

"Umma! What do you mean?"

She answered me in Korean, telling me that when Chris moved to Arizona all those years ago, he met a girl—Megan. She was white. They had been together for over ten years now and had gotten married in Bali. None of us were invited. But we weren't supposed to take it personally. We didn't even know when it was happening. When I asked my mother about it, she simply responded, "That's just Chris."

"I know," she said, frowning. "When I meet her, I look at her and I know, this is girl who has had baby." She breathed deeply and closed her eyes. My father seemed immersed in his food but looked indifferent.

"Wait, you met her?"

She ignored me. "Baby is Megan's daughter. She is fifteen years old now. *Oppah ehgee kee-who-soh.*" *He raised her this whole time.* I thought back to the wedding, when I met all those people who knew my brother but didn't know I existed. He did it again but to his own daughter . . . but why? Why did we get the same treatment? What did we have in common? First, I considered he wanted to protect us; a big brother didn't want his friends knowing he had a little sister. No, that wasn't quite right, because how would that explain Megan's daughter and keeping her from us, his family? Then it hit me: Megan's daughter would be someone who, by all Korean traditional standards, would not be accepted by the family. So he wanted to hide her from us for as long as possible. And I was someone my brother hated, so he didn't want to acknowledge my existence. We were both sources of shame. It wasn't to protect us. He just wanted to protect himself.

Chris has a daughter. The words struggled to sink in. After all these years, our family still had not learned how to talk to one another.

NAH-BEE-YAH
(BUTTERFLY)

Years went by before my mother and I finally learned how to cohabitate in the same city, but it took a while. My mother had to recognize that I had superseded her as a mother and that I held the utmost power when it came to raising her grandchild.

When I was a teenager, my mother would say I knew nothing. She would say she had over forty years of life experience and I didn't know what was best for me. I never revealed to her the harm, the damage this mentality would do: that, to my knowledge, she never knew what it meant to be an Asian American woman. Because if she knew how to navigate this country, she would have shared her knowledge, and she would have supported me through multiple sexual assaults. I was more worldly than my mother because I saw humanity's ugliest traits. But she was never there. My mother was absent despite always hovering over me.

It finally came to a breaking point one day when we had a screaming match outside of my house. It was a disagreement over how to raise Gabriel. And I vividly recall my mother bending over to snatch my baby boy and running down the street. I ran after her, but it was too late. She threw him in the back seat of her car and drove off.

I stood standing in the street, watching her car peel out of the parking lot. *Do I call the police? Do I teach her a lesson?* The same questions my younger self had asked all those years ago. *No. I'll wait.* So I did.

When evening fell, my mother finally returned my son. And then I refused to let her see him for two months. And that is when she realized who held the power in our relationship. She was torn apart. She was beyond upset that she had missed crucial stages of his babyhood. And I coolly stood by, reminding her who had the control to remove access to seeing the one person she truly wanted to see.

The way my mother was with my son made me feel . . . strange. It's a feeling that resembles jealousy, but the definition of jealousy would imply that I wanted something that my son had. No, that wasn't it. I didn't want my mother's affection as an adult. Those days had passed.

I just felt *bothered*. Because I couldn't understand why my mother was infatuated with my son and gave her love to him freely when she openly denied it to me during my youth. It felt like there was a riddle that I couldn't solve, a riddle that I was ready to understand, but someone refused me the answer key.

What I didn't understand then was that gender plays a massive role in a Korean mother's love. Boys will always be treasured, while girls will be treated like time bombs of pregnancy and stupid mistakes. Which is ironic, considering my mother used to forbid me from having sleepovers because she expected girls were up to no good at slumber parties and were sneaking out to have sex. At the same time, she didn't have a single conversation with me about sex and consent.

I suppose if I were more optimistic, I could choose to believe my mother's love for my son had everything to do with me. The reason why she was so entrenched in his infancy was because it was her chance to redo all the things she regretted with me. Maybe.

It took months of passive-aggressive behavior and months of pretending my mother and I didn't have a blowout, yet all the while still being angry with each other. But one day, I woke up and I felt . . . nothing. No anger, but also no forgiveness. No love, but caution. Because at the end of the day, the scorpion always does what a scorpion does, even at the cost of its own life. When I accepted that I could never change my mother and it was more about learning how to manage her, the mental load of our relationship became easier.

When the anger from our fight had subsided and was put in the past, I did something incredibly out of character for me: I called her for support.

One day I was staring at the wall behind the bed. Gabriel was a toddler. There was something about having a child that made me, once again, furious to live, furious to give him something better than I had ever had. Furious to be a better mother than my mother ever was to me. I had everything I had ever wanted. But an inexplicable dark cloud settled over me. *No one will miss me if I just disappeared.*

The emergence of this thought, my thought, surprised me. Ryan was at work, and Gabriel was in school. And I was sitting on the floor next to the bed, staring at the wall. Optic White was the name of the paint color. I was picturing the cleaning up that people have to deal with when their loved ones used guns. But I had also heard that people defecate when they try to overdose on medication. I shook my head. It all sounded so *messy.* The logical side of my brain told me there would be no way I would ever commit suicide, since I wouldn't want to leave behind a mess to clean up. Before

I even knew who I was calling, I picked up my phone and called the one person whose voice I needed to hear: Umma. My mother used to say something in Korean that translated to "You hold nothing in your heart," meaning that I wasn't capable of holding back anything I am feeling or thinking.

She picked up my call after two rings. After I finished telling her I was having depressive thoughts, she sighed, completely unsurprised.

"I worry this happen. I worry my depression pass to you when you in my belly." She went on to tell me that she remembered when she was pregnant with me and she was standing at the top of a flight of stairs. She had a sudden whim to throw herself down the stairs to kill herself. "I take medicine now for my depression." I raised my eyebrows. For some reason, it didn't seem like my mother to accept help, no matter how necessary it was. Because to accept help meant acknowledging there was a problem. And this was not something I could see my mother doing. "Joan . . . I used to cut myself. Doctor in Korea say I have depression."

This wasn't a revelation to me. I had always had an underlying suspicion, but it had never been confirmed. But what *was* surprising was that she had known for that long, when she lived in Korea all those years ago.

"I so thankful that Gabriel turn out okay," she continued.

What does my son have to do with this?

"Joan, remember? *Nah-bee-yah, nah-bee-yah?*" Her words prompted a memory of the time my cousin and his mother came to visit.

He was frolicking around my living room. My eyes followed his movement in total disinterest.

"*Nah-bee-yah, nah-bee-yah,*" he called out in a singsongy voice. His arms flapped up and down, and he chased my cat around the house. The only thing that appeared odd to me was that he was a few years younger than me, maybe nine years old. He seemed a bit old to be behaving that way, but I dismissed the thought as soon as it came, because what did I know about little kids? His mother gazed at him, and my mother laughed.

"So cute!" she said. She then told me to go play with him. I shot her a "You're joking" look. *How do I play with him?* I looked at my cousin again, galloping and giggling as my terrified cat frantically looked around for a place to hide. It looked like he was doing fine on his own anyway. I ignored my mother.

My cousin was intellectually disabled.

My mother continued to explain in Korean the conditions that we might be predisposed to in our family. There was depression on her side of the family, alcoholism and intellectual disabilities on my father's. And she never told me. She never told me when I was pregnant and running all those standard tests to see if Gabriel would be healthy. She never told me when we were bouncing around names for my child. Instead, she chose to sit and wait to see what would come. Because that is my mother: forever wanting to defer pain as long as humanly possible, in the hopes that I would never have to worry at all, because everything would turn out okay. Everything comes out in her own time, with the core belief that she is doing something good for me. She's the gatekeeper of all family secrets. It was my dead cat all over again.

We never missed annual checkups with the pediatrician, and Gabriel tested negative on his autism screening when he was an infant, so I felt reassured that we were passed over. But it would always be in the back of my mind. He would eventually make it into his school's gifted program, much to my relief.

"Lucky Gabriel turn out okay," my mother had said, pleased with herself for sparing me any grief, had she disclosed this to me earlier, when I was pregnant.

"Yeah . . ." I said thoughtfully at her choice of words, knowing it didn't matter to her how I felt in that moment and wondering what lengths she would go to delay my pain. "Lucky."

My mother saw herself as a savior, not understanding that she was still attempting to control my life, my narrative, by withholding information that I was entitled to. And she would ration out morsels when she felt it was appropriate.

The month prior, she was watching my pet rabbit while Ryan, Gabriel, and I were out of town. My rabbit, Pauline, escaped one night, and all indications pointed to him being eaten by a coyote. My mother didn't tell me for a week, because she wanted to delay the news and prevent me from being upset.

My mother has a strange grasp on the concept of grief. She feels as though she is able to wield it, make it shorter. In her mind, delaying pain means you are sadder for less time because the incident was further back in your past. Is there something to this?

If we learn of a death, and it happened a while ago, would we be less sad? No . . . it's upon discovery that the wound opens and we are plunged immediately into grief. My mother's way doesn't work, because ignorance means you never get a chance to grieve. And what she was attempting to remove was the process of grieving. Grieving is what lessens the pain. Grieving is what heals the pain. Without grief, pain is relentless.

What I never understood was how she could play such a risky game. What happens on the day when she makes a critical miscalculation? Will my father die quietly, only for her to give me the news months later? Even then, I couldn't see her being remorseful for her choice to hold back. Because I was assuming getting the news of someone's death would be the highest price I would have to pay for my mother's miscalculation. But Korean immigrants who have fled war-torn countries are friendly with the idea of death—which would mean my mother would never understand why getting the news of someone's death so late would be so egregious.

On some level, I understand why my mother plays this game of withholding information. I, too, don't want her to feel sad about things in the past. To this day, I still don't know my own grandmother's name. And I'm not sure if I ever will ask my mother the name of her umma, a trigger that would send her back into her grief.

But I did know one thing for certain: my mother's game was a firefight, random gunfire splaying from the skies.

I was lucky, indeed, to have dodged a bullet.

THE KOREAN
MATRIACHY

After Gabriel was born, Ryan's parents visited us annually in Seattle to spend time with their grandchild. During their visit in May of 2015, when Gabriel was two years old, I made reservations at an upscale steak-and-seafood restaurant in a suburb outside of Seattle. His parents were staying with us, so we all rode there together. My parents arrived shortly after. As I walked up to my parents in the parking lot, it struck me how strange it was to see both of them together out in public. And how, still, it was strange to see my father at all. He was still working two jobs: five days a week at one job and a part-time job on his two days off.

My father was wearing a beanie over his bald head and a dark blue-and-green flannel under a gray tweed blazer. He'd had that blazer for as long as I could remember.

"Look at Appa!" my mother hissed under her breath but loud enough for my father to hear, while looking at him scornfully. Her eyes were dripping with reproach. "See how he dress like beggar so he won't get mugged on bus!" She rolled her eyes and scoffed.

My father had a bus pass for over thirty years. He didn't know how to drive and had no desire to. Instead, he would spend his spare time riding the metro to wherever he pleased.

For example, he'd spend the day in Canada and return home in the evening for dinner. He was like an outdoor cat.

"You look great, Appa," I said defiantly. Of all the things my mother taught me, she taught me to be defiant. He smiled at me. One time, I had snapped at my mother and told her to cut it out, that she was picking on him like a vulture picking a carcass. She gasped and was so offended that I would take his side.

We were finally seated inside the restaurant at a long booth. The walls were amber colored, and candles graced the tables with a low and ineffective glow. The menus offered drinks such as Manhattans and old-fashioned highballs served with a single giant ice cube.

Ryan, Gabriel, my mother, and I sat on one side of the booth, while Ryan's parents sat on the other. Appa was an unusual guest. And my in-laws recognized this immediately. They fired questions about his background—his childhood and how he came to immigrate to America. I deeply appreciated their genuine curiosity. He rarely got to be the center of attention in our matriarchal family.

Appa didn't miss the opportunity to regale us with stories of growing up in Japan and then moving to Korea during his adolescence. But it's important to note that the only reason he had a chance to speak was because my mother was having a side conversation with Ryan; she was too distracted to see the attention my father was getting. My mother usually finds his stories embarrassing and dismisses them as soon as she's able, concerned that he will bore present company with things they're not interested in. But, like a typical immigrant who is drenched with too much humility, my mother had miscalculated—she discounted the fact that Americans find our stories fascinating. Because our stories are what distinguishes us from them. My in-laws were hanging on every word that fell from Appa's lips.

"My dad speaks German," I bragged.

My father took the prompt and said something in German to demonstrate.

"Oh!" Ryan's stepmother raised her eyebrows. "How did you learn German?"

"I studied it in high school," my father responded, shoveling a forkful of his food into his mouth.

"Oh, wow, that's impressive . . ." She looked at Ryan's father. "I studied Spanish in high school, but I don't remember any of it."

"Yeah, well, my father traveled the world and was a bouncer on a cruise ship for some time," I explained. I understood their skepticism. He did live an unbelievable life. He would sail port to port, and because he didn't have any proper papers or enough money for a place to stay, he would sleep on beaches before the boats would sail out.

"Ah, now that makes sense," both Ryan's stepmother and father said, nodding.

But then I remembered something. "Or . . . Appa, were you a bouncer or a dishwasher on a cruise ship?" I asked my father.

"Both," he answered.

I started feeling a little bit sheepish, because I felt like he was pushing it and I knew he liked adding some flair to his stories.

When we finished eating, we walked together out of the restaurant. We reached the parking lot, and my parents went to their car.

"We never get to hear your dad speak!" Ryan's father commented in amazement.

"Yeah! We haven't heard him talk much. He has such interesting stories!" Ryan's stepmother agreed.

"Mm . . . yeah, he never really gets the chance . . ." I said ruefully. *Was it really so obvious to everyone else that my mother keeps my father in check? Did I really never notice it as a child?* As we drove home, the car filled with their conversation. I sat in the back, looking out the window. It hit home that my father was the foil of my mother. She never shared, while he was always aching to. I wondered if she felt the need to try to keep a tight lid on him because she was afraid that he would burden us with something by accidentally spilling a secret.

I thought back to the year I was at the base hospital in Alaska getting a checkup for my pregnancy. I stopped by the coffee stand, and I ordered a latte from two Korean elders. They bustled around the coffee bar, quickly frothing milk and pulling shots. However, when the man reached over to grab the pitcher of milk, the *ahjoomah* swiftly smacked his hand. Without even blinking an eye, she grabbed the pitcher herself to continue to make my latte. This action represents my parents' relationship in a nutshell. Although society perceives Asian women to be submissive, serving the patriarchy, in our household we lived under a matriarchy. Compared to the presence my mother takes up in our family, there is no space for my father.

ORIENTAL

When I was in middle school, I used my allowance money to buy a Mother's Day gift. I had picked out a hand cream from Bath & Body Works that claimed to help with stress. I thought she needed it. I remember feeling a swell of pride when I asked the cashier to gift wrap it.

When I handed it to my mother, she held up the lotion and scolded me. She was disappointed and disgusted that I had wasted money on a gift that she didn't care for. She made me return it. Other than that one incident, I had no recollection of spending a single Mother's Day with my mother.

Now it was my fifth Mother's Day as a mother. Gabriel, Ryan, and I were eating breakfast at an IHOP, Mother's Day 2016. It was important to me that my family knew that I was easy to please—unlike my mother. When we were done eating, Gabriel and I walked to the restroom while Ryan went to pay our bill. As we were on our way out, an elderly couple sitting at a booth stopped us. They must have been in their seventies.

"Your family is beautiful!" the woman said. She had short, white curly hair and wore large acrylic glasses.

Surprised at her random kindness, I replied, "Thank you!"

"Our son adopted an Oriental," she explained.

Somewhere in my mind, I heard a record scratch.

Her partner nodded enthusiastically. He had snowy white hair, and his face crinkled as he smiled.

"And he's just beautiful," she continued.

"That's nice," I said, smiling, almost touched that they felt compelled to connect to us because we reminded them of their beloved grandson. "Have a great breakfast."

On the drive home, I couldn't help but dissect the encounter. They were at that age where archaic language was almost . . . well, not acceptable but understandable, mainly because of their age. And I knew they meant no harm, but if it was anyone belonging to a younger generation, they would have gotten an earful from me because they should know better.

However, what distracted me most in that car ride was my feeling of being called something so outdated. And the reaction I had was so entirely different than that summer I went camping and was called a Chink, which was a punch to the gut. The word the elderly couple used to describe Gabriel and me felt so bizarre: "Oriental." I knew that Oriental was an offensive, outdated term. Many liken it to the word "Negro" for Black people. I had never been called Oriental before. I had only read about this term, which carried so much emotional baggage for others who endured during a time of legalized racial segregation. The word is associated with incarceration camps and the Yellow Peril.

But for me?

The images that came to mind were of pagodas and Cup Noodles. *Is this normal?* I thought. *Shouldn't I feel angry?* There was a strange disconnect between knowing it was offensive and feeling like I was called a type of rug.

I could only determine that these feelings were a result of being called a term that is so wholly disconnected from today's society that it borders on the realm of absurd, or even obsolete. And I knew it was a result of my age. It did not trigger me, because I was too young to have experienced any racism or propaganda that utilized the term "Oriental." For me, modern-day racists aren't using their 1950s dictionaries to find racial slurs to throw at my face. So if I had to guess what type of person would call me "Oriental," it's going to be Grandma Sally, drinking her iced tea on her porch while asking me if we finished the railroad yet.

When we arrived home, Gabriel and I went upstairs to his bedroom to discuss what Oriental meant, how it used to be used, and how it is inappropriate.

"Our country has had a lot of good and bad things happen," Gabriel observed.

"Yes, it has," I agreed, wondering how a child could hit it on the head so easily while the rest of the country struggled to understand that it is possible to believe in multiple truths.

KONICHIWA!

The mall was one of my favorite places to take Gabriel to get his wiggles out. I would only go on weekdays, when I could enjoy the serenity of the stay-at-home moms and the elderly mall walkers. But today was not one of those days.

"*Konichiwa!*" a man yelled at me from across the mall. Gabriel jumped slightly from surprise.

"I'm *Korean*, you idiot!" I hollered back, without missing a beat. Gabriel looked up at me, his eyes big. I continued walking, holding his hand. I huffed, rolled my eyes, and shook my head. "Come on, buddy. Do you want to go get some lunch?" I asked, tugging him along nonchalantly, his mouth still slightly open.

We walked over to the bagel shop where we were supposed to meet my parents for lunch. This was a common occurrence. After we ate, Gabriel, my parents, and I began walking over to Target to kill time. But on our way, a man mistook my father for Chinese and asked, in Mandarin, where the Target was. For a moment, I didn't know if it was offensive, because this man was Asian. But then I determined it wasn't the same thing as if he were white and asking this way.

What happened next shocked me.

My father responded to the man in full conversational Mandarin. I watched him, baffled.

He caught my facial expression when he turned back toward us. "It happens all the time; people think I'm Chinese," my father explained, not addressing the real source of my confusion. But these days, my parents never seemed to surprise me anymore.

"Joan, you didn't know Appa spoke Chinese?" my mother asked, amused.

It doesn't occur to either of them that I cannot know the things they do not tell me. *How am I supposed to get to know my father when he never gets a chance to talk?* I asked her silently.

I took a mental inventory of everything I knew about my father. I knew that he was born in 1943 in Japan. When the Japanese colonized Korea, they transferred Koreans to Japan to work as laborers. My father's family was among them. At one point, he worked on his uncle's silkworm farm. When they eventually returned to Korea, my father's mother abandoned him and his sister after deciding motherhood was not for her, and his father died soon after of liver cancer. My father took on the role of his sister's unofficial caretaker, despite being only a few years older, and they lived on the streets as orphans. My childhood was peppered with stories of him surviving on the streets of Korea. There was pride in his voice when he would describe the conditions he overcame in his adolescence.

When I was around five, my father got a phone call saying that his mother had been located. He had found where his mother was living, a small town in Korea. He flew out from Seattle to see her, but when he arrived, he discovered that she had died a few years prior. Instead of being able to confront his mother for abandoning him and his sister, he had only his memories left to confront.

The situation with the Chinese man and my father made one thing glaringly obvious: the question of nationality is a complicated one. How many times has someone come up to me asking, "What is your nationality?" only for me to say, "Korean"? If one were to look up the definition of "nationality," it would actually be most accurate if I were to answer, "American," since I am an American citizen—I was born here. America is "my nation." But the problem is that what people are trying to ask me is, "What are you?" I was shocked to realize that my father's nationality is actually Japanese and Korean, not just Korean. But that doesn't answer the question of "What are you?" Occasionally, people asked it correctly: "What is your ethnicity?" But even that question falls short.

If we recognize how complex the conversation around nationality is, then why *wouldn't* this Chinese man assume my father could speak Mandarin? It would make sense, if how you look has nothing to do with nationality, if your ethnicity has nothing to do with where you were born and raised. When we ask the question "What are you?" we are attempting to root around for information so we can make assumptions about your character, about your culture. We don't truly understand the complexities of identities, and that how we look has nothing to do with who we are.

But, above it all, a greater question nagged at me: "How well do I know my father?" I would learn years later that he picked up conversational Chinese while working at Uwajimaya and speaking with his coworkers in Mandarin. And I never knew. I never knew that, quite possibly, my father was the most interesting person in our family.

THE MODEL MINORITY MYTH

I t had been two years since we first moved to Washington from Alaska, and Ryan had been employed at Boeing the entire time. When we initially moved, he and I agreed that I would be a stay-at-home mom until Gabriel started kindergarten. Childcare where we lived was around $1,300 a month, and we didn't want the majority of my paycheck going toward that cost if I could stay at home with the baby. But being a single-income family proved challenging.

The plan was that while I wasn't working, I would focus on getting my Washington State teaching certificate by taking night classes at a university in Seattle. When Gabriel started school, I would get a job at a local high school, and we would be on the same schedule: same hours, same school breaks. It was a perfect plan.

But the reality was that our family needed income to supplement Ryan's paycheck. So I got a part-time afternoon job at the same university where I was getting my teaching certificate. After my shift would end around five o'clock, I would walk across campus to my evening classes.

I worked at the university for a year, but after all this time, I couldn't figure out why my manager seemed to despise me. But then I read Malcolm Gladwell's *Outliers*. The book had become renowned in our city after the Seattle Seahawks made it the first one they read for their book club. When I read the chapter about Korean Airlines, I understood what was happening at work.

According to Gladwell, Korean Airlines has a sterling reputation today. However, decades ago, their planes kept crashing. Korean Air hired a third-party contractor to research what was going on. It wasn't until the contractor found one black box from a plane crash that he realized the answer was a total lack of communication—a lack of cultural competency. What the black box revealed was a conversation between a copilot and a pilot.

The thing about Korean culture is that you have to understand two things: the way we communicate, and our own social hierarchy. Age and position would grant someone the most respect, unlike American culture. This is important to consider, since in this case, the pilot would get more respect than the copilot. It didn't matter if they were chummy, and in this case, it didn't matter if the pilot was older than the copilot, because positionality would trump age.

The copilot, noting the ominous weather, warned the pilot once—something along the lines of "Sir, that weather sure looks threatening." The pilot agreed, then went about his business. The copilot tried again: "Sir, that rain looks pretty nasty." The pilot grunted, or something similar, in acknowledgment but then returned to his tasks.

The plane crashed.

What the contractor discovered was that, in Korean culture, the onus of communication is placed on the listener—not the speaker—which is the exact opposite in American culture. The pilot dismissed the heeding of his copilot, because he wasn't really listening. And the copilot, didn't understand why his pilot was not understanding what he was saying.

After I read this chapter, I wondered how many messages my manager ignored and whether she really knew what I was telling her, and how many times someone else got credit for my ideas in a meeting after I had just shared them. All because no one really knew how to listen. And no one was culturally competent or understood my cultural lens.

At the university, my manager's name was Valerie. And on my first week of work, she had me sit next to her office desk and listen to her speak for four *straight* hours, for three days in a row, about how to use their electronic system. One-on-one, just staring at her face while she stared back at me, rambling on and on about how to use their computer system. Once, I actually nodded off and fell asleep while she was talking to me. And no matter how much I indicated to her that this teaching style did not work for me, she plowed through.

Valerie did not have the patience for different learning types and let me know it. Whenever she spoke to me, it reminded me of the way people spoke to my mother. If Valerie had to repeat anything, she would raise her voice and speak slowly, as if I were hearing-impaired. This felt like a punch in the gut with a hot iron fist.

Valerie only gave verbal instructions and lost her temper whenever she had to repeat something. When I tried to advocate for myself, asking her to repeat instructions for me to write down, she quickly grew frustrated and angry. But what I noticed early on was that when my white colleagues asked her for help, she used a different tone of voice. She would patiently repeat instructions and was noticeably warmer with them than she was with me.

I've seen this before. The model minority myth meant that there were high, almost impossible standards for Asian Americans. This myth perpetuated the fallacy that assimilating into white culture was easy, because Asian Americans were doing it so well—obtaining higher education and wealth while becoming doctors, making immigrating to America look easy. And if Asian Americans are doing well, that means we don't experience poverty and we don't experience racism. This myth erases my experience. Due to my learning struggles, when I didn't fit the model of being high performing with very little assistance, I was met with hostility. Because, to some, I was either that type of illustrious Asian, or I was that type of person of color who couldn't hack it.

It was about a year into the job. As a department, we were all sitting in an unused classroom on campus one evening at our weekly staff meeting. I was working in the admissions office while I was getting my teaching certificate to eventually work as a high school teacher. The fluorescent lights made me feel like I was in a hospital as they gloomily flickered on and off. Valerie, our manager, was standing at the front of the room. She had fiery red hair, pink skin, and a gap between her two front teeth. I had been butting heads with Valerie a lot that week. She ended up screaming at me in the office, where there were rows and rows of cubicles and listening ears. I was humiliated and furious at the lack of respect. She was angry because I had sent an email through our electronic system that outlined the steps a student had to take to get financial aid.

"How could you get it wrong? You sent it . . . and it was wrong information!" she shrieked. I argued back, certain that I was not mistaken. This fed her anger, which flared up and detonated in the office.

Afterward, I scrolled through the emails that my other colleagues had sent. Our electronic system allowed for multiple people to respond to numerous emails at once. This way, multiple people could handle the admissions email account. Since we all had a shared email account, this meant I had access to everyone's emails. I pulled up several emails about financial aid sent by my white colleagues, and they had all given the same information I did. Why was I held to a different standard? Why was I expected to work with very little help? Why was I treated with such little dignity in the workplace? Not only that, but I had been struggling with her being so much younger than me, since in Korean culture, the expectation is to respect those who are older than you. It's a culture in which you would call someone a different title based on whether or not that person was older. I was almost ten years older than Valerie, and she always spoke to me like I was an idiot.

Valerie had begun a new morale program that month. Each week, a person would be nominated for their contribution to the department and receive the Achievement Award. It was kind of like Employee of the Month, but it was every week. As the weeks went on, each employee won this award—except for me. That night, when I was sitting in our weekly staff meeting, it didn't escape my notice that I was the only person of color in the room and the only one who had not received this award. I assumed that, tonight, I would get it just based on process of elimination. I half listened to Valerie spouting off the agenda and waited patiently for the meeting to come to a close, when I knew Valerie would announce the award recipient.

"Okay, everyone! It's time to give out this week's Achievement Award! I'm so excited to announce this week's recipient. This is someone who has been there for every single one of us, has been a shining reminder to stay positive, and brings light into all of our lives." I couldn't believe what I was hearing. Given Valerie's distaste for me, I was surprised she was saying all these nice things.

"This week's winner is . . ."

I waited patiently for her to call my name.

"Falcon!" The staff began to applaud. I was stunned. Falcon was the name of our office fish. Valerie brought him in one day, absolutely tickled at the thought of us having our own office mascot.

I slumped down in my chair, refusing to make eye contact with anyone. I was the hardest-working person in that office, and I never hesitated to ask for help, which I knew Valerie hated. I had made it a point to be outspoken and suggest new ways to try to improve the efficiency of the office.

The next day, I walked into the office and back to our department. There was a small table that greeted everyone before the cubicles began. I saw that Valerie had propped up the certificate next to the fish tank. I gave the burgundy fish a dirty look and then looked around the office. I found a rogue bottle of cleaner sitting on a desk. I picked it up and shook it, confirming the gentle sloshing. Without missing a beat, I unscrewed the lid and slowly poured the remainder of the cleaner into the tank.

Afterward, I marched to Valerie's cubicle and gave her my two weeks' notice.

KIMCHI RAGE AND INTERSECTIONALITY

After I quit my job at the university, I buckled down on my studies to obtain my Washington State teaching certificate. And in six months, I was rewarded, in March of 2017. I quickly got a job teaching at a high school, and it astounded me how easily I was able to get hired. After all, I was a Boomerang Generation survivor and remembered the 2008 economy crash way too much.

My first four years of teaching went by quickly. It was fulfilling, but I started noticing a pattern with how I was treated at work. I couldn't get away with the same things as my male colleagues. Allegedly, the math teacher would cuss at the kids. Another would tell a student she wasn't cut out for anything other than working at McDonald's. Yet I would teach students about race and culture, and I would have parents complaining to the principal about my curriculum. Once, a mother demanded a meeting with the principal and me to complain that I was teaching slave narrative in class. My course was American Literature, and I was teaching Frederick Douglass's works. She stated that her daughter did not feel safe being a Republican in my class and that I was anti-white. She also loosely threatened me with a lawsuit, bragging about the fact that she had gotten a settlement from a school district in downtown Seattle.

I looked her up later, and indeed, she had won a very rare reverse-racism case against a public school in the nineties. She was awarded just over a million dollars.

The odd thing was, I collaborated closely with another teacher in my department. She never got a single complaint. The only difference between us? She was white. I was not.

One afternoon, I stayed after school for another meeting with the principal. I had been teaching for a couple years, and the new school year had only been in session for a couple of months. We had been in the principal's office for what felt like forever. I looked at the clock. It had been forty minutes since the principal started verbally reprimanding me for being "aggressive." A white male colleague had complained about me because, during a staff meeting, I had strongly expressed my disapproval at the way authors of color were being taught by our department. One teacher expressed more concern with getting through as many authors of color as possible, instead of taking the time to do them justice. I believed in having conversations with the students around how an author's racial identity impacts their texts as a central discussion.

The principal was still going on about my inappropriate behavior. I realized I was too Korean for this predominantly white space when he said he wanted me to apologize. *Don't you mean apologize for being a strong Korean woman?* I thought. The intersectionality of my identity frequently puts me in this position, in which being a bias disrupter and defying American expectations of meek, submissive Asian women resulted in people constantly labeling me "aggressive." While the principal continued, I thought about pointing out that what he actually was doing was mislabeling a Korean woman based on stereotypes that he had long accepted.

Do I bother to explain? Do I try to explain the culture and historical context of Korean women and our strength that is always perceived as "aggressive" in America? Do I explain what Korean history and generational trauma had to do with the strength of the Korean people? That, as a result of the Japanese colonization of Korea, the Koreans did what they could to survive? Do I explain that when the Japanese soldiers abducted Korean women to be their sex slaves, the Korean women still endured, and their strength lived on? That Korean books were burned, the language banned to conquer not only Korean land but Korean minds, but we still endured? After all, I still see evidence of generational trauma, as my mother still says with disgust, "Japan never even apologize for how they treat us!"

And add intense national poverty on top of that. Through endurance and grit, the fierce Korean spirit survived. It is actually referred to as "Kimchi Rage" and has a separate word in Korean: *han*. In fact, it was known that the Japanese drove large metal spikes into Korean mountains, believing that they could kill the spirit that survived in the mountains that fed the people strength. But as my white principal continued to insult me, I decided it wasn't worth it and that one conversation would not change a white man's implicit bias on race and gender.

"I'm sorry," I said absentmindedly. He nodded his head in satisfaction. I slightly hated myself for it, and I wondered if I made the right choice to give him what he wanted. In that moment, I had inadvertently fulfilled his expectations of being a submissive Korean woman. And in that moment, I felt disgusted and disappointed in myself that I had been so weak.

If I could redo that moment all over again, I would have tapped into the gift that my mother gave me: the gift of defiance. Although not all hills could be hills to die on, I knew even then that I missed an opportunity to make him sorry for questioning my identity, and for putting me in a box labeled "Quiet Lotus Flower" and slapping my wrists when I wandered out.

I should have screamed discrimination. I should have made him sorry. There was already so much literature around the Angry Black Woman but barely anything about the Angry Asian Woman.

You don't fuck with the Angry Asian Woman. Similar to how the Angry Black Woman is dubbed thus for being deemed "aggressive" for only being assertive or outspoken, the Angry Asian Woman is deemed "aggressive" when she is not the submissive sex slave men want us to be, like in the movies.

MICROAGGRESSIONS

After my meeting with the principal, I tried to lie low in my department to preserve what little fire I had left. The first few months of school flew by, and before I knew it, it was Thanksgiving break, 2018. Ryan, Gabriel, and I had flown out to Oklahoma to visit Ryan's family. They lived in a city where I had almost become accustomed to being one of the very few people of color around.

Ryan's niece was six years old. I was sitting on the floor, braiding her blonde hair. I didn't have a daughter, so I quickly accepted when she asked if I would play with her hair. That afternoon, the family had invited a friend and her husband over. Without thinking, I spoke to Ryan's niece lovingly in a Korean accent as I was brushing. After a lifetime of hearing my family speak in that accent, I went in and out of it fluidly around my friends, but then again, my friends were mostly Asian. I realized my mistake the instant I said it. The white neighbor excitedly chimed in.

"Do you want to hear mine?" she asked eagerly.

"Hers is *really* good," her husband said. Before I could interject that my accent was not an invitation, she threw the dart at me.

"You want gel nayyyyls? You want geyyyyyl?" she drawled in mockery. My stomach and eyes burned, but I stared ahead and continued to brush the little girl's hair.

Later that evening, Ryan's father was excited for us to eat at a hibachi restaurant in town. When we arrived, we sat in a circle around the grill and marveled at the presumably Japanese chef chopping, flinging, and flipping food around in front of patrons' faces. Everyone oohed and aahed on cue. But something suddenly caught my ear. I heard the fakest Asian accent at the table behind me. And when I whirled around to throw an accusatory glare, I stopped suddenly in my chair. The man was another Asian chef, who was playing up the worst, most synthetic-sounding Asian accent I had ever heard.

"You wan' flied lice?" he called out over the sizzle and clinking of scraping spatulas. He sounded like Mickey Rourke from *Breakfast at Tiffany's*. We locked eyes. And I did the only thing that came to mind: I narrowed my eyes in disapproval, maintaining eye contact, while slowly shaking my head in disgust. This Asian man had sold out; he had submitted to being a sideshow for the entertainment of white people. "If you can't fight 'em, join 'em," I could almost hear him say. I knew exactly what he was doing. He was capitalizing on a stereotype that our people had to suffer, on their perception of our stereotypes. I couldn't inject any more fury into my glare that criticized his disservice to our people.

The cook looked down in embarrassment.

APPA'S SECRET

After our return from Oklahoma, Ryan was still elated about how well the vacation went. I didn't share my experiences or observations, since I didn't know what to make of it yet. And because the Sung family didn't know how to communicate with one another, I was never gifted with that ability.

Ryan wanted a chance to live in the same city as his dad and strengthen their relationship. One day, he decided on a whim to relocate the whole family to Oklahoma City's Boeing. Although living in Oklahoma didn't appeal to me because of its lack of Asian American representation, I was open to it because it meant I could once again live away from my mother.

I told my mother and father that we were thinking about it. My mother gave all the reasons under the sun why it wouldn't work, which made my desire to get away from her even stronger. She called my brother, and he called me, accusing me of being a traitor to the family since it was my responsibility to take care of our parents in case anything happened. Never mind the fact that he lived several states away and never once offered to take care of them if they got sick or too old to care for themselves.

Almost one month later, I got a phone call out of the blue. When I looked down at my phone, I saw "Mom." My stomach still lurched when I saw her name come up on my phone.

"Umma?" I said tentatively when I answered.

"Appa is dying," my mother said abruptly. She didn't sound sad; she sounded resolved.

"What do you mean?" I asked, thinking I had mistaken what she meant.

"He has autoimmune disease. His liver is bad," she said. "Medicine is too expensive, insurance won't cover. This happening for a long time. He got it long time ago and still fighting."

"What autoimmune disease?"

"Hepatitis C. He used to . . ." She paused, searching for the words in English, but resorted to Korean. *Sell blood? Blood transfusion . . . sell plasma. For money.*

"Appa had hepatitis this whole time? When?"

"Many years ago. When you were little. It bad now. Appa has been drinking," my mother continued. It was as if waves continued to crash onto me, and I was powerless against them. She was talking in a tone that sounded like confession, which led me to believe that she had been holding out on me for quite some time. "He hide drinks under the bed and secretly drinking and getting drunk," she elaborated. "His liver is ruined, and it doesn't help the hepatitis. Doctor say he make it worse." And there it was. As she finished filling me in, I realized she was telling me, without telling me, that my father was a drunk. Maybe not an alcoholic, but a drunk.

My father's drinking initially came as a shock to me, because he was such a devout, old-school Christian and so disciplined. It didn't seem like him. But maybe it came as a shock to me because we were more alike than I thought. *Like father, like daughter,* the little voice in my head whispered.

My mind suddenly flashed to a forgotten memory from early childhood when we were still living in California. I must have been two or three years old. It showed up like a photograph in my mind. My father, with a full head of hair at the time, sat on our apartment balcony, drinking a beer and smoking a cigarette. I didn't know what that memory meant, but on that day, on the phone with my mother, I thought, *Maybe, on some level, I did know this entire time* . . .

"Umma, why didn't you tell me this earlier?"

"I don't want you to worry, be a burden," she said quietly. This again. "I don't want you to worry while we figure out what to do. And if we figure it out, then no worry at all!"

"Umma, you have to stop this. You can't keep holding off on telling me stuff. It's so much worse when you wait!"

"I understand," she said. I knew she didn't mean it. I was also suspicious of the timing of her sharing this piece of news, knowing that it would oblige me to stay home in Seattle. I didn't doubt my father was sick. And I trusted that she'd been holding out on the news to delay my pain once again. But I suspected that she knew what she was doing when she chose then to share my father's diagnosis, soon after I shared that Ryan and I were considering moving to Oklahoma. I knew her timing was well planned in order to keep her hooks in me.

The doctor gave my father a year to live, unless he was able to get a hold of the hepatitis medication, which cost about $150,000. We didn't have that kind of money. My mother had attempted to get the medication covered with insurance, but they denied the claim. Once my brother heard what was going on, he swooped in. That is, after he reproached my mother for never telling him what was going on either. He insisted on flying them out to Korea, where health care was cheaper and they could pay for the medication outright. My mother refused and said she would keep submitting the claim with the insurance company. So she did. Over and over again, her claim was denied. Then she would immediately resubmit. Until one day, a few months later, the claim was approved. I could only assume after giving into my mother's tenacity, the insurance company caved. My father's life was saved. The price tag for my father's life went from $150,000 to $15.

When I think about my mother's tendency to defer her children's pain for as long as possible, I wonder if she looked at this entire situation as a waste of sadness. She must have seen it all as an unnecessary encumbrance that didn't have to happen, since my father's life was saved in the end. After all, it was only when my father was essentially given a death sentence that she divulged. This showed me how far she would go to protect us. But the lengths my mother would go to protect my brother and me from grief would prove, time and again, to be the worst kind of nuisance.

KOREAN BARBECUE

Since my father was cleared of his disease with the medication that insurance finally covered, Ryan and I quietly picked up our discussion to move to Oklahoma. I was still unsure, and something in me protested. I called my girlfriend Amelia for advice.

"We're thinking about moving to Oklahoma," I said slowly.

"Why?" she exclaimed.

"Ryan's dad . . . Ryan wants to spend more time with him . . ."

"But your parents are older; they'll need you sooner," she countered. And I knew she was right. Despite the fact that I didn't want my mother to feel like she was right, the reality was that my father was in his seventies—I had limited time left to spend with them. Ryan's parents had him at age nineteen; his grandparents were the same age as my parents.

I also knew that Amelia's opinion would be rooted in our culture. She was Chinese and knew all about filial piety. Parents come first. Duty comes first.

"I just don't want my mom thinking she is the reason why I'm staying . . . that I'm listening to her advice," I whined.

"Joan, sometimes you just have to take the path of least resistance," she said, laughing.

I sighed. She was right. I knew the answer was right in front of me all along. I couldn't move to Oklahoma with my biracial son, to live in a place with untrustworthy politics.

"Anyway." She changed the subject playfully. "If Gabriel is going to be an Asian cowboy with an accent, you should come to my going-away party—it'll be a dual party. Your going-away to Oklahoma and mine to San Francisco."

"Sounds good. When?"

She texted me details. It was a Korean barbecue in North Seattle, in Shoreline. It was a good opportunity to push everything troubling me to the back of my mind.

Most of our friends came, and most of us were Asian, but I was the only Korean to attend. One of our friends, Liz, an elegant girl who had the composure of a ballerina, had spent a few years in Korea teaching English. She was, I felt, more Korean than I was, despite the fact that she was white. Her conversational Korean was impressive and gave mine a run for my money. I didn't even know how to use chopsticks properly, which was always a source of embarrassment. As a little girl, I had just figured out how to use them my own way, and my mother never corrected my form.

When it was time for us to order dinner, my Chinese friends immediately prompted Liz to order for the table. I wasn't the least bit offended, because they all knew I didn't feel comfortable speaking Korean to people outside my family. But when the Korean server approached the banquet table, he immediately approached me and waited for me to speak. I looked up at him looking expectantly at me, holding up a pad of paper and a pen, nodding his head to show he was ready for me to begin.

"Erm . . ." I wriggled in my seat. Liz was sitting on the other side of me and waved them over confidently. Without hesitation, she shot into a stream of Korean and ordered for the entire table. I picked up on all of my favorite dishes that she was ordering. I felt a mixture of relief and shame. Before the server walked away, he stopped by my side once more. "Do you want to add anything to the order?" he asked in Korean.

"What she said." I smiled, my face burning hot, while I sunk into my chair.

WHAT DO ASIANS HAVE TO DO WITH RACE?

The COVID-19 pandemic arrived with an aggressive swiftness that none of us could have anticipated. Like 9/11, most of us could remember where we were when we learned about lockdown. I was teaching in a classroom of seniors.

My students were on their cell phones. Not an unusual occurrence, but they never liked to see me go "full Korean," as we called it jokingly. I looked around the classroom, gawking at all the cell phones that were out.

"What is this?" I cried. "Are you *new*?"

My students didn't move an inch.

"Hel-lo? Can you hear me?" I raised my voice.

Emma, a stellar A-plus student, was also on her phone. Her jaw was open, and she dropped her phone in her lap. "Mrs. Sung, schools are shutting down," she said, stunned.

"Nooo," I said skeptically, dismissing her statement with the wave of a hand.

"Oh my God, it's COVID—people are dying right now, it's super contagious, and it's deadly," Michael, another student, said, panicked. Everyone began stirring in their seats, and the uproar started.

"Hey! Hey! Quiet down, everybody!" I shouted over their voices. "Listen . . ." I waited for silence. They looked at me with eagerness, their eyes pleading for me to reassure them. "It's just a flu virus! We'll all be fine!"

Their phones chirped. Their heads went down once more. "Mrs. Sung . . ." Emma started. My breath caught in my throat, because I knew by her tone what she was about to say. "Our school just closed. We're supposed to go home." It was March of 2020.

We were told lockdown would be two weeks. Then three. Then my seniors never got to see the stadium they were supposed to graduate in. No winter formal, no prom. No parties, no pep rallies. No football games where a select few would show up drunk. Kids were robbed of their first dates, their first kisses. It was all wiped from their futures and replaced with fear—and first masks, first Zoom meetings, first banana bread loaves, first sourdough starters . . . first experiences of racism.

On May 25, 2020, George Floyd was murdered. And the entire country heard a community shriek in excruciating pain and rage. The news flooded with flames, canisters of gas, and broken glass.

"Look at those Black people looting. Wouldn't expect anything less."

"This is just no excuse for violence. Those poor business owners . . ."

"Why aren't they listening to Martin Luther King Jr.? Isn't he supposed to be their hero? MLK said no violence! What a disgrace."

What else are they supposed to do when they have tried everything else to get this country to listen? I thought dismally as I read the comments online. But at the same time, I wasn't surprised.

George Floyd's murder also triggered something complex between the Black and Asian communities. While some came together in solidarity, others remained cautious, fulfilling white supremacy's agenda of pitting Black people and Asians against each other to fulfill the model minority myth.

What became evident to the general public was the lack of education around Asian American history. What public schools weren't really teaching was that when the Chinese Exclusion Act (which impacted all Asian Americans) was repealed and immigration laws ever-so-slightly loosened up, America began screening Asian Americans for who would be worthy of allowing back into their country. They skimmed the cream of the crop and granted citizenship to Asians who were doctors and lawyers. Once these "high-performing Asians" were allowed into the country, white supremacists began parading these model minorities around, rubbing their successes in Black people's faces, with the point of saying, "See how well these immigrants are doing? Why aren't your people doing just as well?" This sentiment gave birth to and fueled bitter Asian–Black relations. This is despite the fact that Black people were never even immigrants to begin with, were not provided with government resources after the Emancipation Proclamation, and were expected to, as Martin Luther King Jr. said, "pick themselves up by their bootstraps." Impossible.

Even popular Hollywood films such as Spike Lee's *Do the Right Thing* and Albert and Allen Hughes's *Menace II Society* depict Asian and Black tensions. These tensions reflect white supremacy's aim of pitting races against each other, buying into the belief that the other is the enemy, rather than racism. And the sad truth was, there were many from the Asian

American communities who also bought into it, who played right into it.

And although several films that glorified the pitting of Blacks and Asians against one another were produced in the eighties and nineties, resistant attitudes pushing against solidarity still held true today. In 2020, I began speaking at national conferences on Asian American advocacy and fighting against Asian hate. I always opened the remaining twenty minutes up to a Q&A. The comments never failed to surprise me. And I always got the same one: "How are you not taking away from the Black community when you talk about Asian hate?"

Because it's not pie. There is enough freedom from oppression to go around. It's also not an us-versus-them mentality. We can both work toward something without being pitted against each other in the Oppression Olympics.

When COVID-19 vaccines became readily available and the public slowly began to open up again, I attended a book reading hosted by a fellow author I knew. The reading was in the tourist hub known as Pike Place Market. The sun was beginning to set on the normal bustle and was suddenly the perfect backdrop for a zombie apocalypse as stores began to close. It was March 16, 2021.

Along with the civil and racial unrest that punctured the facade of America after the murder of George Floyd, that morning a headline punctured my soul. It was about the Atlanta salon shootings, in which a white man assassinated eight people in a massage parlor, six of whom were Asian American women. The shooter claimed he was getting rid of his sexual addiction and temptation. But the reality was that he bypassed numerous strip clubs to target Asian-owned massage parlors. It was the sexual fetishization and stereotypes believed about Asian women that led him there.

Much to my dismay, rumors spread like wildfire on news outlets stating that the women in the massage parlor were prostitutes. But our communities knew that they were just *ahjumas* who were trying to get by in this country. It didn't matter; the damage was already done. And a law enforcement officer had reported to the media that the shooter was just having "a bad day." A bad day is a paper cut, a failed test, spilled coffee down your work uniform. We Asian women were expendable because we are not people; we are objects for white men's sexual objectification and desires. We are easily scratched out as collateral damage on someone's bad day.

On the streets of Pike Place, there was not a soul in sight. I should have been used to the diminished crowds after the pandemic, but after that morning's news, I was on high alert. I read somewhere that Asian hate crimes had also increased over 400 percent in the past year. The statistics were alarming, but the sentiment was not new. We had experienced hate this entire time: Yellow Peril; the Chinese Exclusion Act, which impacted all Asian American Pacific Islanders; the Japanese American internment camps; Vincent Chin . . . and so much more. But the exponential spike in public assaults and public murders was shocking. I began feeling the tightness in my chest again, a feeling I had not experienced since the military.

I could hear my shoes click against the cobblestones. I glanced down at my phone once more in desperation, trying to figure out the directions. I was trying to follow Google Maps to find a small hidden library in the heart of Pike Place for my friend's book event. But my GPS was glitching, and before I knew it, I was completely turned around.

"You have arrived," Google Maps announced. "You have arrived."

"I have not fucking arrived!" I whispered fiercely. I groaned and threw my head back in frustration. I took a deep breath as my mind wandered to the events earlier that day at home.

I was sitting in a chair across from Ryan, and I was crying so hard I could barely speak. He reached out to me with his words, over and over again. But nothing was enough. I looked at the man I had married. Did we know what it meant to be in an interracial marriage? Did we really know?

"Have you seen the news? Do you know what they are doing to people like me? Like Gabriel? You haven't once checked in on me . . ."

Ryan looked helpless. And he was retracting into himself. I could see it. His eyes averted, and his tone became a bit duller. He hates confrontation. And his reaction made me sick to my stomach. I could feel myself losing respect for him. And based on what I had seen of my parents' marriage, without respect, a marriage begins to curdle.

"You have nothing to say to me?" I said venomously, feeling like a wounded animal lashing out.

Ryan looked down. We were oceans apart. And I hated him for it.

Ever since the start of the pandemic, I had told my parents to speak Korean in public a little quieter, to consider carrying around pepper spray. Anti-Asian hate crimes had spurred throughout the nation, and Americans were just becoming aware that Asian Americans were also subject to racism. This is after decades of believing that we also held privilege, that we were perfect specimens of the model minority. It was as if the country didn't realize that Asian Americans were also people of color, and until the violence against the Asian American community was covered on the news, we were considered to be just like white people. But the glaringly obvious evidence of American history indicated otherwise: our people had to endure anti-Asian racism for centuries. Time and time again, we are thought to be exempt from racist incidents since we aren't Black. But at the same time, we are not white enough to get privilege in white spaces.

Ryan and I were feeling tension in our marriage as a result of the hate crimes. I no longer felt safe venturing out, since the crimes were completely random. Ryan was beginning to shut down and retreat into himself because he didn't know how to support his Asian wife and son. I was beginning to doubt whether I truly thought through the implications of an interracial marriage.

How will you support our biracial son when he gets called a Chink for the first time? How are you preparing yourself?

He had no answers. I pointed out that after the Atlanta massage-parlor shootings, he didn't even check in with me and, at minimum, ask if I was doing okay. He was at a loss and felt like a failure. He became more and more quiet on the subject because he was terrified of saying the wrong thing to me. In my eyes, he had become one of those silent, complicit white people. "If you can YouTube how to fix the plumbing in our house, you can google how to be a better ally," I told him. He finally understood that the one thing he cannot do is disengage from this conversation. I began doubting the sustainability of our marriage.

One day, when another attack on an Asian woman had splashed across social media, he came home from work and sat on the couch with me.

"Are you okay?" he asked. I became overwhelmed with emotions and tears, relieved that we were finally moving in the right direction. "I promise I will do better, and I will find a way to support you guys," he said.

"I'd better see you researching this as much as I see you researching the next car you're going to get," I declared.

He looked at me earnestly and nodded his head. He saw what was at stake.

As I cried on our couch, I could finally see him on the horizon.

The one subject our society is not discussing is exactly this: the impact of these anti-Asian hate crimes and what it is doing to interracial marriages. There may have been a day when we could ignore the other person's race and just be happily married partners. But that time has passed. Now we must brace ourselves for the reckoning within our own marriages, because these racial tensions have infiltrated our one safe space: our home.

I was so deep in thought as I walked through the streets of Seattle that day, looking for my friend's book event, that I didn't realize I was being followed. A man was walking quickly behind me, gradually closing the distance between us. I quickened my pace. I slipped my hand into my jacket pocket and clutched at my pepper spray, which I had just ordered on Amazon.

From the sound of his footsteps, the man broke out into a brisk jog. *What the fuck?* I thought in a panic. My hands began to sweat. I whirled around to face him.

He was now within a few feet of me. I stared at him in stupor. Terror gripped me.

"I've been watching you running up and down this street! Are you lost?"

I did the only thing I could in that moment: I fell to the ground. I wanted to cry, but I had nothing left.

The following week, Ryan and I invited our neighbors over. After showing our negative COVID test results, we safely unmasked and shared a meal. But quickly, we began arguing about white privilege over dinner, a conversation prompted by discussions of George Floyd's murder. One of our neighbors was insisting that they don't have white privilege, because her white husband grew up poor. I clarified that white privilege did not mean that you led an easy life. It was not about what you went through, but about what you didn't go through because of the color of your skin. Then I continued on to say that I didn't want their skewed perspectives on race to be projected onto my biracial son, and that if they felt a certain way, to please keep their opinions about race to themselves.

"But he's half Asian. You're Asian. What does any of this have to do with you?" she demanded. I thought, *That is the issue. Because if you ignore the racism toward Asian Americans . . . you can go on simply ignoring what is happening to us.*

WHAT'S IN A NAME?

My mother refers to Korea as "my country." She always says how she and I are fiery because we have North Korean blood that runs through our veins. She remembers the region before the times of dictatorship and Communism. For her, it is frozen in time when her mother was alive, before she fled from Communism.

"Long, long times ago in my country . . ." is how her stories begin. I always felt as though my mother emigrated from Korea against her better judgment, as if there were some regrets. I knew she felt like an outsider in America and at some point hoped to return to her home country. "But I won't belong there either," she would say sadly. "I gone too long." This helped me to understand why she never committed too much to learning English, why she never socialized too much with those outside of her Korean community: it was the place where she felt most at home. She had rejected assimilating to American culture, because her assimilating would mean losing a part of herself, and she refused to let that happen.

For example, if an immigrant wants to have an easier time assimilating to American culture, it is standard to pick a new name, a name to go on all your official citizen documents, such as your passport. What no one talks about is the loss of identity that happens when you give up your birth name to pick an American one that is easier for Americans to pronounce. My father picked "Bill" when he arrived. I used to think my father chose the easy way because my mother, my proud Korean mother, kept her Korean name, "Moon." As a result, she spent her life yelling in some American's face, "No! My name is Moon! Like sun and moon! Sun and moon!"

My name, Jo-won, means "good" in Korean. Or so my mother tells me. Growing up, the other church girls were given separate, traditional Korean names that weren't based on the way their American name sounded, like mine was. I was embarrassed that mine had such an inauthentic ring to it, since it was just a phonetic pronunciation of an American name. As the story goes, my mother said she had always loved the name "Joanne." And when she gave birth to me at Queen of Angels Hospital in Los Angeles, it came time to give the nurse my name. "J-O-A-N," she had spelled. When the nurses began calling me "Joan," my mother was puzzled, because she had wanted my name to be Joanne. But she shrugged her shoulders because she liked "Joan" too, especially because it sounded like "good" in Korean.

When I was thirty-four years old, I finally had clarity on how my mother felt about names. I was setting up my mother's Internet account, because she didn't speak strong enough English to speak with customer service. They informed me that all requests were done online now, and all that my mother had to do was register and set up her email. My mother and I sat at her computer as I began setting up her account.

"Umma, you need a username," I explained to her.

"Username?" she asked, puzzled.

"Yeah, it's like a name, a nickname that you have for your account."

My mother nodded in realization. "I know! Helen!" she suggested.

"No . . ." I started to say but thought again. "Okay," I responded, wondering where the name came from.

"I always wish I pick Helen when I come here to America. Such nice name."

"Okay, Helen it is." I set up her email for HelenSung. Her choice revealed how, if she could have done it all over again, she would've picked the easier way and preserved her dignity rather than dealing with a lifetime of people mispronouncing her name.

WHITE OR BLACK

t was January of 2021, Martin Luther King Jr. Day, and the COVID-19 pandemic continued. I read Gabriel the same book I always did this time of year: *Martin's Big Words*. Gabriel was in second grade, and school was still on Zoom. But while we were reading, I recalled a particular year when I read him this very book, back in January 2019, when he was in kindergarten.

That evening in 2019, everything played out as it always did. Gabriel and I were in bed, and we were snuggled under the covers getting ready for bedtime as I read from the book: "Sooner or later, all the people of the world will have to discover a way to live together."

After I turned the last page, I closed the book and kissed him on the forehead.

"It's so sad we did that to Black people back then," Gabriel said somberly. I understood that all of us held implicit biases and needed to hold ourselves accountable to do better for racial equity. But the way Gabriel said "we" made me pause. For some reason, I was picking up on a misunderstanding buried in his meaning.

"Wait, why do you say 'we'?" I asked.

"What we white people did to Black people back then," Gabriel explained.

"But, honey, we're Asian!" I blurted out, surprised. I stopped myself and reconsidered my feelings. I suppose I had never considered the complexity of Gabriel being half Asian and half white until this moment. He certainly wasn't white passing, as the only thing he inherited from my husband was his cleft chin. I wasn't sure how to approach this conversation. What was challenging was raising a mixed kid without being mixed yourself. Yes, my son is Korean, but I was aware of the harm of raising a mixed kid as full, because it erases the other side of their heritage. So, up until this point, I had coached Gabriel on his Korean and German ancestry. But even when he spoke about what his white ancestors did to Blacks, there was something else that was bothering me; I couldn't shake the fact that I felt as though he was missing something else in his understanding.

"I mean, yes, you are half white . . . but you know you're Asian too, right?" I said.

"No, Mommy. I'm white. There are only two races—white and Black," he said matter-of-factly.

And there it was.

"Who told you that?" I was shocked. After all the times I spoke to him about our heritage, about my parents' immigration stories . . . it wasn't enough. I had discounted the capital that public education had on the impact on a child's identity development. Public education did not do enough, and at the same time did plenty to erase my son's racial identity; in one fell swoop, there were only two races in existence in America in the narrative of many children of color in the United States. The polarization of the Black–white experiences in the way we talk about race in this country continues to erase the experiences of Asian Americans.

"Those are the two races we learn about in school," he explained.

This can't be right, I thought. "Don't you guys learn about Asian holidays?" I probed.

"Oh! I forgot—Chinese New Year." An afterthought. And, of course, a Chinese holiday. Because everyone thinks we're all Chinese. And when Americans think about the term "Asian American," China is the only one they think of rather than the other over fifty cultural groups in Asia.

I pulled up an infographic of different children's faces on my phone. There were about nine different profiles of cartoon children, all varying in skin tone and all from different heritages.

"Which one do you think you look like?" Passing his finger over the faces of the children, including the Asian one, Gabriel's finger landed on the white child. I was incredulous.

"Wait, why?"

"Because I have white skin. See?" He pointed to the back of his hand.

"Um . . ." I was at a loss. The complexity in this conversation astounded me. It was so much bigger than my son or me. But at the same time, I knew that this conversation could not end in determining that he was just too young to understand.

"I have white skin like Daddy," he persisted.

I stayed silent, feeling helpless. And it dawned on me the lack of preparation I had for raising a mixed child. "But, baby, we're also Asian. You're not just white."

To my surprise, Gabriel erupted into tears. "So we're Black? But that means we were treated so bad by people! Like in the book!" He sobbed, horrified at this new, inaccurate revelation.

I took a deep breath and gathered my wits about me because I knew I had to intervene. "Gabriel, listen. First, there are way more races than just white and Black. Being not completely white does not automatically make you Black. You are German and Asian." I brushed his bangs across his forehead with my fingertips.

"And there are way more types of Asians, like Korean. That's what you and I are. This"—I pointed to my phone—"is what you and I look like." Gabriel gazed upon the little Asian boy. "It is not just about matching your skin color but about what country your ancestors come from. Like *Halmonee* and *Harbojee*. They flew on a plane here from Korea. Okay?"

"Okay," Gabriel said slowly.

I could tell he was struggling to reprogram. "Oh, and Gabriel?"

"Yes?" he answered.

"You are not just white. 'White' does not belong to a country. You are German. Daddy is German. It's important you know your heritage. Okay?"

"Okay, Mommy."

I reflected on why that felt important to me in that moment to correct him in identifying as white.

The thing is, it is not problematic to raise a child to believe he is white, but it is severely problematic to raise a child to believe he is *just* white. White is not a culture, not a nationality. That term was originally meant as a way to label a superior race, to champion over Blacks during segregation. White is a social construct that was created to justify a behavior and a mentality. It's a dangerous game to coach a child to embrace his whiteness.

Because when we do this, and when these white children grow up and are inevitably asked to define their heritage and their culture, they are only left to claim America as their country. Which reinforces the idea that this country is theirs, and the rest of us are all visitors. But I was also born here. This is my country too.

White power and white nationalism are not movements that celebrate their heritage, because it doesn't exist. Since they had no cultural roots, they claimed bits of our cultures as their own through cultural appropriation and built a fake culture that is only a few hundred years old. As a result, what they are celebrating is a history of racism and oppression. This is why it is important to teach children the origin and the country of their ancestry, not their skin color.

So when my son is celebrating his heritage, I refuse to allow him to celebrate his whiteness.

"Tell me again. Where are your ancestors from?" I pressed my son, as we huddled over the book about Martin Luther King Jr. to read it again.

"Korea and Germany."

"Very good, my love."

I remembered that day in 2019 as if it were yesterday. And I looked at my son, who had grown older and had already lost traces of baby fat in his face. I looked at my son, who had survived returning to in-person school, wearing masks, and was trying to have a normal life. I looked at my son, who was once so confused over his racial identity and felt as though he had to "pick one" since public education didn't have enough representation for Asian Americans, let alone biracial Asian Americans.

That day in bed, as I cuddled my second grader, I picked *Martin's Big Words* back up and mindlessly flipped through the pages once more as I quietly reflected on our conversation a couple of years earlier. And I wondered, as I did every year, if I did a good job of explaining his identity to him. But as I was flipping through the pages, my eye caught a page where Dr. King stood, as a child, in front of a WHITE ONLY sign. The words on the page read, "Every time Martin read the words, he felt bad, until he remembered what his mother told him: 'You are as good as anyone.'"

A mother's words—a child's story always begins with a mother and her words.

As a little girl, I spent a lot of time in the library. One thing my mother was great about was facilitating my love of reading by taking my brother and me there regularly. The library was located right off a walking bridge, where pedestrians could look over the rails into the local river that ran beneath it. Every October, my mother would take us to the bridge to catch glimpses of the salmon struggling to swim upstream.

"Salmon!" I would scream in delight to my mother and brother. My mother would nod encouragingly and excitedly.

Another fall memory was my mother gathering fallen chestnuts on the large grassy field in front of the library. My mother enlisted my brother and me to help and to gingerly collect the funny-looking spiky balls that would fill a repurposed *namdaemoon* grocery bag. She would coach us into identifying which were ripe to take home and which were better left in the grass; when the spikes were a teddy bear brown and tinged with green, they were fine. However, if they were too much of a lime green, let them be. Only when the bag was bulging with our treasures were we allowed to go inside the library to read for an afternoon.

It is only now as an adult that I realize, like the chestnuts, I would only collect memories of my mother that would align and justify my dislike of her. Sadly, her tender moments would be lost upon me when I would soon grow too bitter to remember them, discarded and forgotten like the unripe chestnuts in the grass. What my mother and I didn't realize was that memories had weight; the memories that cause trauma leave a mark—a bruise. They're harder to forget.

My brother would always go straight to the Young Adult section, while my mother could always find me reading *Garfield* comic books and hiding in a little tent that had been set up in the center of the children's section. Out of the many days my brother and I spent in the library, there was one I'll never forget.

When I was in first grade, I settled into the tent to read one weekend morning. But I got sidetracked when I found a children's book titled *Where Did I Come From?* sitting in the center of the floor in the tent. The illustration depicted a baby crawling out of one of the *O*'s. Intrigued, I opened its pages and saw a man lying flat on top of a woman; both were naked. *This is how babies are made*, I thought.

"Sex," I said aloud slowly. The word was foreign to me. I decided I wanted to take it home with me to study it more closely. When I found my mother, waiting in line for Customer Service, I approached her, holding up the book.

"Umma, can we borrow this?"

My mother's face shifted as if I had held out a muddy toad for her to touch. "*Bleghhhh!*" she spat. She snatched the book out of my grasp. "Where did you find?"

"In the tent." I pointed to the children's section.

She strode quickly over to the tent and chucked the book back into it. "That book yucky!"

I was confused. Instead, I walked back over to the tent and carried the book around with me during our visit to the library, dodging my mother. When it was time to go home, she caught me holding the book again, and she took it from me once more and threw it behind the counter. She grabbed my hand and dragged me out of the library, never to talk to me about the book again.

Gabriel and I had just had our discussion about race. And after our talk, it prompted me to peruse his bedroom library. I immediately noticed that all the characters in his books were either animals or white people. So I decided that we would spend the next afternoon at the library to pick out some books with Asian children depicted in them.

He needed to see more representation, more kids who looked like him. I couldn't depend on schools to provide that for him after he determined there were only two races in the world: Black or white.

The next day, Gabriel and I walked across the parking lot at our local library. The sky was overcast and dreary. The rain fell, not in big fat drops, but as a fine mist that was just enough to annoy us. Gabriel jumped heavily, stomping two feet firmly into an ankle-deep puddle. I opened my mouth to scold him, then stopped myself when I thought of my tiger mom. After a lifetime of suffocating parenting, I wanted my son to live freely, with just enough parameters to feel safe. Cold, wet feet would be a lesson to him but also would allow him to enjoy life. Gabriel looked up at me. I smiled before pulling up my mask to step into the library. He did the same.

As we walked through the glass doors, I breathed in deeply. The smell was distinct—dust and musty paper with a lingering trace of isopropyl alcohol cleaner. The room was well lit with natural light pouring in from the tall windows, despite the gray weather.

I didn't quite know where to start, so I approached the librarian, a squatty older woman with gray, unruly hair pushed into a bun. Her eyes crinkled when she smiled, as the rest of her face was tucked behind a mask. When I explained I wanted a book that wasn't about Asian culture but had Asian characters, her expression was—I think—mystified.

"I'm really not sure if I can help you find anything like that..." Her words trailed off as she wandered up and down the aisles, Gabriel and I following her like two ducklings. She finally arrived at the tiniest section in the library.

"But here is the International section!" she said brightly.

"Erm..." I started, trying again. "No, I mean books about American kids, but they're Asian. Not like a holiday book or anything like that, but a story where the character happens to be Asian... Does that make sense?"

Her eyes said no. She didn't understand that we were American, not "international."

"I'm afraid this is the best we have," she apologized. I thanked her, and she soon wandered off.

Eyeballing the International section, which sadly boasted three rows of books, my face fell. I reached out for one book, using a single finger to tilt the title toward me before I grasped the cover with my fingers. When I caught a glimpse of the title, I scoffed.

The title was *The Runaway Wok*. I was dismayed—angry, even. I shook my head. I turned to Gabriel, who was distracted by the other books outside of the International section. "Let's go home," I said.

In 2019, the Cooperative Children's Book Center reviewed 4,075 books and, of them, only 8.7 percent had Asian or Asian American protagonists. And after seeing the so-called rich narratives that were out there, I was critical of even the 8.7 percent. How many of them confined the stories of Asian American kids to only be about Chinese New Year or about strictly international themes or experiences? Especially when there are so many Asian American kids who just want to see themselves depicted as characters who are having average American lives and happen to be Asian? This subtle distinction makes a huge difference.

"STRENGTH" IS LOST IN TRANSLATION

After the library, I took Gabriel to my parents' house. I frequently encouraged this relationship, because I figured time with my parents could help my son feel rooted in his culture—especially since I couldn't expect children's books to do that for him.

That weekend, Gabriel and I sat on the floor in the living room of my childhood home. My dad handed me a Starbucks gift card as he knelt down to sit with us. I looked at him quizzically. "Appa, where did you get this? You don't go to Starbucks."

He chuckled. "Today at work, a lady asked me to help her find a good head of lettuce." He leaned back, waving his hand around the way he does when he's gearing up to tell a story. My mother was in the kitchen, cooking lunch for us. "I give her one. It's no good. I hand her another one. It's no good." He shook his head. "This happen over and over again. She's driving me crazy." He laughed. "Why don't this lady leave me alone, I think. She keep bugging me! She was starting to piss me off!"

I couldn't help but laugh with him.

"She come back up to me and say, this part of this one lettuce is good, but the other side bad. And this one—this side of the lettuce is good, but the other side bad. So you know what I do?"

"What, Appa?" I was completely engrossed in his story, since I rarely heard him speak so many words.

"I take the two heads of lettuce. I take one, I rip it in half, like this." He made two fists, put them together, and made a twisting motion. "I take the other one, I rip that one in half, like this." He twisted his hands again. "Then I take tie and wrap it around two good sides. I say, here! There's your perfect lettuce! And she laughed! She was so happy! Turns out, she was a secret shopper! She said I gave her excellent customer service, and she gave me Starbucks gift card. Now, you take."

I looked down at the gift card. My dad's tolerance astounded me. His whole life, he had been like this—emulating a monk-like serenity and patience, only to turn around and tell me what he really thinks. He had a kind of self-control I admired. And I knew it was somehow different than submission. He emulated strength and discipline, because he refused to let people get to him.

When the COVID-19 pandemic hit us and there was an over 400 percent increase in anti-Asian hate crimes, so many people asked our communities, "Why are Asians so quiet? That's why this violence is happening. It's because you all are so quiet, and people know they can walk all over you."

My father and the lettuce—his little anecdote gave me the clarity I needed. The word "strength" is lost in translation with white Americans.

We Asian Americans are not quiet. Many just perceive us as quiet because of the stereotypes of Asian people— that we're demure, submissive. We fight back; it just doesn't look how they think it should look. The American way of "fighting back" is to be loud, aggressive, combative, to physically dominate over someone else. But when we look at Asian canon literature, such as Sun Tzu's *The Art of War*, we actually understand that our way of fighting back is intellectual warfare, and that to go to battle means to admit defeat. In other words, "Crouch to conquer." Crouch—not bow down. Just because we Asians are not showing rage does not mean we are not feeling it, as it is also a Buddhist ideal to have mastery over oneself to demonstrate the utmost discipline. It's a difference of cultural norms.

And that moment is when I learned of the gift from my father: the gift of endurance and protecting your inner peace, a Buddhist idea to its core.

I looked at my father's aged face. "I wish I was more like that, Appa."

He smiled. "You gotta just ignore, and *whoosh*." He motioned his hand over his head. "Let it fall off you. There are so many idiots."

I chortled. And then my mother walked in. I already knew what she was going to say.

"*Yohboh!*" she reprimanded, like she did when she felt he was rambling and boring the present company.

"Umma!" I shot her a look to leave him alone. I peered at my father's face, but he didn't appear to mind. He was smiling contentedly, staring off into space. I wondered if he was using his own advice to deal with my mother.

That following Monday, I had a virtual interview with an Asian student at the high school I worked at. The pandemic had been going on for a little over a year, and school was still online. I was sitting in my makeshift home office that I had thrown together when schools shut down as a result of COVID. The student worked for the school newspaper. He was doing a story about the Stop Asian Hate movement. His first question was: "Why have Asian Americans been so quiet about the increase in Asian hate crimes as a result of COVID?"

I sighed.

This question again—the question that triggered an overwhelming sense of exhaustion. I was tired of people assuming that because the media did not highlight our protests, we were being stereotyped even further as a submissive group of people. And, as a result, people assumed we were complacent with the rising anti-Asian hate crimes. I felt like I owed it to this Asian student, who still had a lot to learn about the history of the Asian American community, to explain. Before I began, I thought of my father and his advice when the woman in the grocery store harassed him for the perfect head of lettuce. Maybe if I told this kid the problem with stereotyping Asians as submissive or quiet, he would spread the word.

I took a deep breath and began. I told him that the Asian idea of strength doesn't translate properly in English. In America, "strength" means to be outspoken, to be loud, to dominate over someone else. But being a child of Asian immigrants, I understood strength to mean something else entirely: our parents' strength.

And I told him about what my father taught me about strength.

I told him that strength means to pick up and move to a new country and start over. I talked to him about Buddhism, in which strength means protecting your inner peace. About Sun Tzu's *Art of War*. I told him the film *Karate Kid* had it wrong. For those of us like me, who actually studied Asian martial arts, the practice was never about conquering other people; it was about conquering yourself through self-control. Strength is resisting the urge to react with an eye for an eye and to rise above, keeping the end goal in mind. It is not always weak to walk away from someone treating you poorly. It takes strength to walk away with your head held high because you knew the inner strength it took to walk away. I told him strength is *ignoring* nonsense, not to be mistaken with *putting up with* nonsense; I talked to him about my father's gift.

But if I were to speak with that student again, I would have clarified that, as with the idea of multiple truths, somewhere along the way, admittedly, our immigrant parents twisted "crouch to conquer" to "keep your head down to keep the peace and assimilate" because their primary focus became the physical safety of their children. This sentiment became "turn the other cheek," because it was about enduring all injustices in order to win the war. For them, this meant providing their children the opportunity to achieve the coveted American education. Because if not for education, how else would their families rise through the ranks? Winning the war, to our parents, was living our lives well once we made it to the top.

This emphasis on physical security and safety is derived from our parents' love language: acts of service. If we look at what adversities they left behind in their home country—war, poverty, and so on—their ultimate way of telling us they love us is by getting our basic needs met. They want to ensure that we will be fed. Which is why, when you step through our parents' homes, the first question they will ask is, "Did you eat?" But, if you're really listening, they mean, "I love you."

If I could speak to that student again, I would emphasize that everyone had it wrong when they wondered why Asians had been so quiet through decades of racism and Asian hate. Everyone fixated on our parents' misguided efforts to keep us safe in this country, thinking that is how we would react to the violence as our people are slaughtered in the streets in the wake of the COVID-19 rise in anti-Asian hate crimes. But our generation knows better. It just doesn't look like America's idea of strength and fighting back. We're strategizing and planning, because we understand there is more than one way to win this war.

Nonetheless, the student on the Zoom call was grateful I had taken the time to speak with him.

"Thank you for taking the time to explain this to me and to let me interview you," he said.

"This took me my lifetime to figure out," I said with a smile. "I'm just glad I can pass this on to you."

Weeks later, word went around the school that I was open to talking to students about the rising hate crimes against Asian Americans, and Asian students were looking for an adult to vent to. A Filipina student wanted to schedule a virtual meeting with me, and I agreed, curious to hear what she had to say, especially because she wasn't a student of mine.

"I feel like I don't have a place among these protests against Asian hate crimes. I don't feel Asian enough to be included," she lamented.

I surprised myself by smiling. I recognized what she was feeling. I thought back to when I was in middle school, around twelve years old, when kids at school called me "Twinkie" or "banana" because I was "yellow on the outside, white on the inside." But what I didn't realize was that we were never Twinkies or bananas. We were a swirl. Because to be Asian American means to be infused with dual cultures and identities and to be both at the same time, inside and out—it is not one or the other. Those kids had the Asian American identity wrong the whole time. Being an Asian American kid of immigrants is accepting the in-between place where we stand, because we are pioneers of this identity. Our parents moved here from another country knowing who they were, and we were born on American land, set out to discover on our own what it really meant to be Asian American. And accepting our identities meant accepting our Westernized parts and the parts of Asian culture we have adapted and carried over from our parents. How would I explain all this to the Filipina student in my video call? How could I fit a lifetime of reckonings in one conversation?

"Take ownership of your identity. That feeling of being displaced? Like you don't quite fit into either culture? That in-between space is what it means to be Asian American. Take ownership of it. Because that is who you are."

AMERICAN ENOUGH

Months had passed since I met with my students over Zoom, and the conversation had faded from my mind. Summer break arrived, and I became busy with filling Gabriel's calendar up with playdates. But I discounted that even if I wanted to forget how I was perceived in society, society will not allow me to forget my double consciousness. W. E. B. Du Bois once wrote about this, referring to the Black experience, but never knowing how profoundly his work related to the Asian experience as well.

Gabriel was seven years old, and we were having a playdate at the Museum of Flight in Seattle. It was strange to see military aircraft and homages to the armed forces. By then, it felt like my time in the Air Force was a separate life.

The museum was separated into multiple parts; the majority of the museum was in aircraft hangars. The hangars were vast and spacious enough to hold at least twenty aircraft. There were even smaller prop planes hanging from the ceiling, as if they were infant mobiles above a crib. Each aircraft was surrounded by a velvet rope that children everywhere teased, grabbed with their small fingers, and rocked to test limits with their parents.

The family friends we were with had their three children. Ryan was at work. We had spent the entire afternoon running through each section of the museum: World War I, World War II, spacecraft, and commercial aircraft.

When we were done for the day, Gabriel and I stopped by the gift shop while my friend took her kids to the café.

I told Gabriel he could pick out one item as a souvenir for our trip, and he picked out a toy airplane. We walked over to the line to pay. When it was our turn, I asked the cashier, "Do you give a military discount?"

"Yes," she responded, eyeing me skeptically. "For the *United States* military," she emphasized. I paused for a moment, making sure I'd heard her tone correctly. In that moment, I chose to pick up my father's gift of inner peace rather than my mother's gift of defiance. I then fished into my wallet for my veteran's ID and handed it to her with a flourish. She said nothing. When Gabriel and I walked back near the restaurant to meet back up with our friends, I told the mom what had happened. She was outraged.

"You need to send a complaint!" she insisted. But for the first time in my life, I felt peace. I thought of my dad's strength, and again about the woman and the perfect head of lettuce. And for the first time, maybe ever, my "otherness" didn't bother me. I used my father's strength to defuse the experience, because I was finally at a point in my life where I understood my worth. Someone else's opinion couldn't affect me, whereas before it would lead to me questioning my identity. As my father would say, she was just another idiot. It had nothing to do with me.

I looked down at my son, who was busy examining his new airplane. I hoped he was watching how I had handled the situation and refused to allow an ignorant person to trigger me. It was in this moment I realized that I had control over my own reaction to ignorance. Although I will never be able to control how other people react to me, it was up to me to choose the lessons my son will learn, based on how I respond. The world will always have more idiots, as my father would say. But I could control how my son sees me, and I had the power to influence and inspire how he would mimic my behavior. In that moment, I chose my peace. I chose to be the woman I wanted to be, a woman who knew when to speak out and when to preserve my fire. I chose to be the mother I wanted my son to have. I wanted to protect my inner peace, and I did not want my son to see me unhinged, allowing someone to rob my afternoon of bliss with him.

REPRESENTATION STILL MATTERS

In January 2022, my eight-year-old son, my husband, and I were at home, finally watching *Shang-Chi* for the first time. We were sitting in our living room, and tears streamed down my face. There was finally a superhero that looked like my son on TV. What was it I was feeling? Joy? Yes, and . . . grief that I had to wait so long for this moment? Maybe sadness for the child in me, who never got to experience what my son was experiencing in that moment?

My husband was looking at me sympathetically.

"Gabriel!" I exclaimed. "An Asian American superhero! Do you understand how cool this is? Mommy never saw an Asian superhero on TV until now! This is a big deal!"

He just smiled and nodded nonchalantly. It dawned on me why I was crying but my child was not. To him, the representation of an Asian American superhero had already become part of a wide narrative that he had accepted. To him, this was normal, not groundbreaking. He will never understand the depth of how important this moment was. And for that I am grateful.

I thought back to the little girl who taped her eyes to make them look more Westernized—to do anything to have the double eyelid. The little girl who flipped through catalogs, never seeing other girls who looked like her among the pages. The little girl who internalized the message that to look like her was undesired—that being Asian was ugly. But this little boy—my little boy—would know differently.

There was a wet chill in the air, and it was raining in Seattle, per usual. When the movie was over, I was washing the dishes in the kitchen when my cell phone rang. I looked at the name on the screen—my brother. He never called me, and all the news I heard about him came secondhand from my mother. I felt butterflies in my stomach, dreading the discomfort of making small talk with a stranger.

"Hello?" I answered tentatively.

"Hey, it's me," my brother said.

"Hi." I was curious as to why he was calling. I attempted to change the subject. "What are you up to today?"

"I'm drinking," he shared.

Aha, I thought. This explained the random phone call and why he felt compelled to make it. He tends to get sentimental when he drinks and forgets that we're not close.

"I just did Dry January."

I looked at our calendar on the wall. "Chris . . . there's still a week left in January."

"Shut the fuck up," he shot back.

"O-kaay," I responded. *This is going well*, I thought.

"I was thinking . . . we should all go to Vegas together on a trip. You and Ryan, me and Megan," he suggested. He then went on for several minutes about the amenities he was accustomed to in Vegas, since he was considered a high roller. "They get a limo to come pick me up from the airport, and we'll get free champagne."

He was trying hard to convince me, but I didn't know why. I had no desire to go on a vacation with him, and I had already moved on from repairing our fissured relationship—without any resentment, without any ill will. Just . . . indifference. I was simply content with where our relationship was, and I wanted him to be happy in his own separate world. And, to my understanding, he was.

"I'll think about it," I lied. There was nothing to think about.

"Yeah, think about it. It would be fun."

"Well, I have to go make Gabriel dinner. I'll talk to you later." I was ready to end the phone call without a commitment.

"Okay. Let me know about Vegas."

"Okay. Bye." I pushed END on the phone, knowing it would be a trip we would never take.

I paused for a moment before dialing my mother. She picked up immediately.

"*Jo-wan?*" my mom answered.

"Umma! Oppa just called," I said, frowning into the phone.

"Oh?" she said, surprised, but she sounded pleased. In Korean, she asked what he wanted. I told her he was drunk. She sighed and tsk-tsked, in Korean if that's possible.

Continuing in Korean, she advised that we treat each other well, because we are all we have when they die. To this day, I still don't understand this advice. Because I know that I have much more in life than a brother I don't speak to. I wanted to change the subject.

"Umma, can you teach me how to cook *bulgogee* this weekend?" I pleaded—pleading, because I have asked her a million times. In the past, I have reminded her that it was important to me to pass down her recipes to my son—that if she died, her dishes died with her.

She sighed. "Why? You can buy good Korean food now!" she said.

"Umma, I need to learn how to cook it for Gabriel when he gets older."

"Ah. When I dead," she said matter-of-factly.

I laughed, shaking my head. So she did know. "Yes, Umma. Sure. Please?"

"Yes, it's okay. I am ready to meet God. I am not afraid to talk about it. Come this weekend."

That weekend, I drove out to my parents' house with a pad of paper and a pencil. When I walked through the door, my mother was prepping everything in the kitchen to begin cooking; all the ingredients were spread out on her counter-top as she cheerfully rummaged through the refrigerator for the remainder of what she needed. The smell of the house always evoked a visceral response in me; I was back to being a small child. But this time, instead of the smells just being a background scent, the powerful odors of kimchi, barley tea bubbling on the stove, and fermented soy permeated the air and greeted me like an old friend.

"Okay, ready? This much water." My mother showed me a random saucepan filled about a quarter of the way up with water. She whirled around and grabbed a random bowl. "This much sugar," she said, as she shook an unmeasurable amount of sugar from a canister into the bowl. "And ginger. This much," she instructed, as she held out her forefinger, using her thumb to show me how much of her finger I was supposed to measure for. I realized my pad and pencil were useless. There were no measurements to write down.

"Part of a cooking pot filled with water . . . one cup-ish of sugar . . . one thumb tip of ginger . . ." I wrote down uncertainly.

"See bottle?" She held up a bottle of soy sauce. "Use this much. One, two, three, four, five!" She tipped the bottle into a bowl as the soy sauce flowed out of the spout.

I eyeballed how much of the soy sauce was gone from the bottle. "Five seconds of soy sauce?" I wrote down.

After she had finished mixing the ingredients, she took a long-handled silver spoon and carefully scooped at the *bul-gogee* sauce from the bowl and held the spoon to my mouth. "Try. When it tastes like this, it perfect."

I sipped. I had to admit, it was perfect. "So . . . just remember what it is supposed to taste like," I confirmed dubiously.

"Yes. Remember."

Later that afternoon, I told my mother I wanted to go through their closet to find things to show Gabriel—pictures of Umma and Appa when they were young and living in California, my own baby photos. My mother agreed. My father was on a walk through our neighborhood, but I knew he wouldn't mind.

When I opened the closet, I saw a large Tupperware at the bottom of the closet. I pulled back the lid to reveal an emerald-green and gilded photo album. I opened it, and much to my delight, it was a photo album of my father—my father in over twenty different countries, when he was work-ing on the cruise ship that he would always tell us about. Each photograph had a label underneath it that had the name of the country he was in. When I finished flipping through the pages, I set the photo album down beside the Tupperware.

I continued to dig and found an old graduation cap and gown that belonged to my father, and underneath that, an enormous, white three-ring binder. The title read: *Sung Family History*. Something in me clicked into place. A binder filled with our story—our Korean story. Generations upon generations, all documented and transcribed on my dad's typewriter, the same one he had used to write me letters in basic training. I knew then that he had written our family story for me. And it dawned on me that, after all this time when I was searching for answers, I had overlooked the one person in my family who had always wanted to talk.

Among the memorabilia, I found something of mine that I'd left behind when I moved to my first home station in the military: a bundle of letters I had received while in basic training. Sealed in a plastic bag, I recognized the loopy handwriting on the envelopes. I immediately felt shame, shame I had not felt in a long time. Although I had begun to accept my identity and my Korean heritage, I realized that I now had to forgive myself for how I had treated my father. I knew I had not necessarily mistreated him, but I had spent my childhood embarrassed of what he did for a living. I had spent my childhood ashamed of our poverty, when he was doing his best and working seven days a week at two jobs. When he had showered me with love, I had taken him for granted.

I opened the plastic bag of letters. I began pulling letter by letter out at random and rereading them.

March 10, 2010

Sweety Joan,
How have you been?
Your mother and I are fine here.
When you received my letter, you will be finished most of your training schedule. March 20, 2010 will be your last training week?! How did you make all difficult things? You are the best of the bests. You should receive a generous share of praise. We are so proud of you.
How about your dormitory living and foods? Did you have a good room and were you sharing with other soldiers? What was for dinner? Did you have milk, coffee, and other foods at cafeteria? How would you like every thing? If you go to overseas, you will get more better foods than there. My co-American class mates told me that they had better foods than they had in the US.
When I was training in the US Army in 1966, I had the first time best foods in my life. I had experienced in simply starving. We can go back to 1950s. During the Korean War (1950–1953), the crops did not survive the drought. Many Korean people were starved to death. When the war started, I was 8 years old. So, I climbed many mountains and cut cambiums from pine trees. I had eaten them and survived. Those cambium had starches, sugars, and cellulose. Between the wood of tree and its bark, there is a thin band of living, dividing cells called "the cambium." As new cells are formed in the cambium. That is the

old story. Korea is a very much rich country in Asia. You never find that kind of poor story no more.

So you will have good foods in Korea.

If you have good news, call your mom or me.

I have to call your brother and ask him how he is doing.

I am getting old, but I do not worry about you and your brother. Both of you are doing very well. I am so lucky to have you as my own children.

You are a young woman. You are a real Air Force soldier. Still I could hardly believe it. Yet there you were, showing us your real face with military uniform and a machine gun in the picture. God would make you brave enough to go on hard military training, no matter what the difficult things threatened to do. You are such a good child and fine Christian. You prayed to Jesus for help. Your mother and I prayed for you and wrote letters to encourage you. Jesus listen to all our prayers. The most high God! He will continually take care of you in the future. Cling on Him and ask Him for help.

I love you so much.

Take care of yourself.

God bless you!

Love Dad and Mom

I was filled with remorse. I tried to recall the number of times I wrote my father while I was in basic training. I couldn't remember sending him a single letter. When I was struggling to understand who my father was, he had revealed himself to me in a bundle of letters, the most insight I would ever have into my father. I just didn't pay enough attention. I understand now that it is a child's disposition to take for granted the parent who provides their love freely and to hold out for the parent who holds their love for ransom. And my father deserved more from me. He deserved a doting daughter in return for his loyalty, instead of another version of my mother. So I did the only thing left that I could do: when he got home from his walk, I told my father I loved him.

SOHN (HAND)

I t had been almost two years since the pandemic began. Now most of us were no longer masking; the majority of Americans were vaccinated. For those of us who were fortunate enough not to lose anyone, it was almost like a bad dream. Almost.

It was March of 2022. It was still cherry blossom season, and the Seattle area unfolded as it if were Okinawa in 2011—when the cherry blossoms marked the beginning of a new love between Ryan and me. Now, in 2022, it marked the beginning of the chapter after COVID and celebrating another year of my life as a mother.

But with the petals that decorated the sidewalks in pink confetti, there was also a smattering of dead leaves. It was a rare dry afternoon, when rain was something to count on in March in Seattle.

Ryan, Gabriel, and I were out on a walk in our neighborhood. Gabriel was riding his scooter. Whenever his wheels rolled over the fallen leaves and made a crunching sound, he would exclaim, "Cunch! Cunch, cunch!" It was a little homage to what he would say when he was small and struggled to enunciate his *r*'s. He knew it made me laugh. As Gabriel rode his scooter, he would occasionally hop off to squat and examine a lone snail or worm on the sidewalk—exactly the same as he did when he was a toddler. It wouldn't be long before he fell behind, and Ryan and I walked a little ahead of him.

As Gabriel caught up to us, approaching me from behind, he slipped his hand into mine, happily riding with one hand on his handlebars.

"Your hand is warm!" he exclaimed. And just like that, I remembered a moment from when I was a little girl.

"Sohn!" I would call out to my mother, reaching my arm out. My mother would slip her hand into mine and squeeze my palm. "Umma, your hand is *ddaddateh*!"

She smiled. "When you have warm heart, you have warm hands, Joan."

It was a memory of a conversation that happened many times. The time and place were elusive, but I knew it was a special bond we had shared, almost like a rehearsed moment between the two of us.

And I knew then. I knew that all the anger I had held on to as an adolescent did not allow me to see my mother in her entirety. When I had reached for her hand, I was asking, "Do you love me?" And when she reached back, it was her way of saying, "Of course I love you."

THE BEGINNING

Ryan and I were on a party bus headed from our hotel to a wedding venue in Fairfax, California. It was Memorial Day weekend of 2022. The Seattle weather had followed us there—gray skies, intermittent rain. Given the earlier bout of heat mixed with the unexpected storm, there was a heavy humidity in the air that lingered between the drops of rain.

I watched the drops begin to hit the windows of the bus before I turned to my friend's boyfriend, Keith. Ryan was sitting with another one of our friends elsewhere on the bus. Keith and my girlfriend had been dating for almost two years, but this was my first time meeting him. He was thirty-six years old and had a goatee, a bald head like my father's, and a crooked smile that made him look twelve years old. I deliberately sat next to him so I could get to know him better. As we discussed his relationship with my friend, he began to share the dynamics of their relationship and how culture played a role: both he and my friend were Chinese.

"Don't you feel like our parents' cultures influence us a lot in terms of the way we are in our relationships?" I ventured.

"Oh, absolutely! And it wasn't even as if I was ever outright taught our culture; it's just things I picked up on from my mom."

"Yeah, immigrants tend not to tell us long stories about their upbringing or anything like that . . . I feel like we just kind of have to infer," I agreed.

"In my circle of friends, we did this exercise where we shared our backgrounds, our cultures. My turn was coming up, and I was so nervous."

"Were you really?" I exclaimed. I was touched that he felt this exercise was so important. I was also enthralled that a group of friends would take the time to share their stories— that they would find culture so important in terms of getting to know one another better. I wished I had done something like that with all of my friends.

"I spoke to my therapist about how to even go about finding out my parents' immigration stories, when they're not exactly open to sharing them," Keith continued. "What she told me is that it's more about gathering pieces of what you already know. Like, what details do you have, you know? And then you string them together. Because there are things that we somehow know, whether through vague references or general impressions from our parents. And once we put those together, we have something that resembles a longer narrative that we were never told directly."

I fell silent. I mulled over this for several minutes. And it was then when I realized how important it was for one to start at the beginning when finding an identity. Because I don't know where my parents end, and where I begin. To my annoyance, people always ask me why I never asked my parents directly for their immigration stories or about their time living in Korea when there was nationwide poverty. I don't think they understand that it's obvious to us children of immigrants that our parents don't want to talk about it. So we are inadvertently trained not to ask. I rarely pry into my parents' pasts. I don't ask follow-up questions when my parents finally do share little tidbits of their stories, the reason being that I am just grateful that they shared anything at all. At the same time, I'm afraid to trigger some trauma that my father says "we already grind up into sand." I understand what is really happening when my parents open up: they are rationing their stories in order to avoid plunging into unspeakable sadness. But without the details and the essential context, I was left struggling to define what it meant to be children of immigrants on my own.

For the remainder of the bus ride, I thought about what I would present if I had a turn in Keith's friend group to share my family background.

I knew the story of my mother's escape from North Korea, and my father's birth in Japan as a result of colonization. But only because I had done exactly what Keith was describing: I had pieced it together over the years by collecting fragments and inferences.

What I knew of my parents' immigration stories is that my parents didn't know each other when they lived in Korea, but both happened to be teachers. My father eventually got off the streets, went back to school, and studied hard enough to earn two bachelor's degrees. But when he immigrated to America, those degrees didn't amount to anything, and he had to start his life from scratch. My mother immigrated to America shortly after my father, to the same city in California where my father was living. Both my parents were in their thirties and struggling to find someone to marry, so they separately approached their church pastor to set them up with someone, anyone, who belonged to the Korean church. It might be said that my parents' marriage was nothing short of an arranged one. They met briefly, right before the wedding, and that was that.

After marrying and having my brother and me, my parents moved us to Washington in 1991, allegedly to escape California's earthquakes, after a freeway bridge collapsed onto itself near where we lived. I was four years old. My parents barely spoke English, and it was a miracle that Quality Food Center (QFC), a grocery store, took a chance on my father and offered him a job as a produce clerk. This was a vast improvement, given that my father, a few years prior, had been arrested in Los Angeles for peddling sunglasses on a beach without a business permit. My mother worked briefly in a sweater factory, and I vaguely remember walking through rows and rows of braying sewing machines and the unidentifiable scent of mixed fabrics. I strongly suspect she worked in a sweatshop. Eventually, my mother quit to raise my brother and me.

There were only two words that came to mind when I reflected on my parents' immigration stories: "immigration trauma." It was immigration trauma that had become generational trauma. There was once a time when I asked my mother if her mother ever shared the trauma of fleeing her own country. My mother laughed dryly and said sarcastically, "'Trauma'? What is this word? What a joke. We didn't call it trauma, because that was just life."

THE APOLOGY

When Ryan and I returned from the wedding in Fairfax, the weather was unchanged in Seattle. The trees were gnarled and bare once more to give way to fall. Then, before we knew it, it was Christmas 2022. My husband and I had just purchased our first home, using veteran's benefits. Despite what I had endured during my time in the military, I was utterly grateful to the Air Force for giving me financial opportunities I never could have afforded. I knew that my decision to serve in the military had broken a cycle of generational financial struggles. And now my son was going to grow up in a house with stairs, something I remembered as being a sign of having money. Ryan and I weren't rich by any means, but we had enough, which was more than I ever dreamed of having.

In our living room was a cheap plastic Christmas tree that Ryan had purchased for me from Target when we were twenty-four years old. It was the first Christmas tree I ever had. And year after year, when Ryan would insist on replacing it, I would tell him that I could never get rid of it, as it reminded me of what I didn't have when I was younger; it reminded me to stay grateful and to remember the days when I would pray for the things that I had now.

Ever since we moved back to Washington, we would host my parents for Christmas dinner. This Christmas, my mother was sitting on the floor, hugging Gabriel as he read a book. She looked up at the tree, and much to my surprise, she said, "Joan . . . *meeyanheh*." She was sorry? For what? In Korean, she continued to explain that she was sorry that she could never afford to buy my brother and me a Christmas tree and Christmas lights, because we didn't have the money.

"I thought you were going to say you were sorry for how hard you were on us." I laughed, nervously, hoping to wheedle an apology from her. "I mean, look at how you treat your grandson now, Umma. You were so much harder on us."

My mother was quiet for a moment, before saying, "Well, he is grandson. That is different."

I shook my head. "Remember when Chris dropped to his knees in front of you, like he was praying? One time he had done something wrong . . . and he begged you not to hit him?"

Silence.

I cautiously continued. "And you did? You started smacking him?"

To my shock, my mother bowed her head. With one hand, she pulled her glasses away from her face a few inches, and her other hand reached behind the lenses to wipe her eyes. *Oh my God. Was this it? Was this the moment she would apologize? Is this the acknowledgment I have been waiting for?*

"Stop, Joan. *Noomoornah*." If I had to roughly translate to the best of my ability, this does not mean "I am crying." There is a different phrase in Korean that means "crying." *Noomoornah* would more closely translate to "Tears are coming." And this nuanced translation was important to me. Because, of course, my mother would not admit to crying but simply acknowledge that emotion was arising. And I knew that this was the closest thing to an apology I would ever receive. And it was enough.

In that moment I remembered the advice she gave me when I was pregnant with Gabriel—to only have one baby because "two is too many." It was then I realized that my mother had two kids when she probably should have had one. Ultimately, her parenting was why I decided only to have one child. Instead of fantasizing about the size of my family, I wanted to make sure I had the number of kids I felt I could handle, so I could be the best version of myself as a mother. I wanted to make sure I had the capacity to give my child as much of myself as I could without growing resentful. And she gave me this advice because she understood that she had failed me on some level as a mother.

My mother's "advice" was her way of expressing how she was sorry. So, in that moment, sitting in front of my Christmas tree, I forgave her. For the lashings, for the harsh words, for the lack of tenderness . . . for holding me up to an impossible standard. And after that moment, I never looked at her again with the resentment I had carried through adolescence, because for the first time in my life, what little she had to give me felt like enough.

ASIANS DON'T SPEAK UP

Ryan, Gabriel, and I were at Coulon Beach in Renton, Washington. Gabriel and Ryan were at the playground, and I stood near the water by the docks. I watched as the waves gently rolled in, causing the ducks and seagulls to bob up and down as they paddled under the surface of the water.

I was eating a sandwich, and the waterfowl clamored near me, hoping I would take mercy on them. And they predicted correctly. Instead of eating the last of my crust, I tossed it carelessly into the water. But what happened next, I could not have predicted.

A mother duck lunged for the crust, presumably for her ducklings. Surrounding her were about ten of her new hatchlings. When she lunged forward, she moved away from her brood, and a seagull saw an opportunity and took it.

When the mother duck was distracted, the seagull descended and snatched a duckling's neck between its beak. I watched in horror, in confusion, thinking that this meant seagulls were carnivorous. But the seagull wasn't hungry. Instead, it continuously plunged the baby duckling under the water, then picked it up to shake it violently between its beak, like a dog with a chew toy. The duckling eventually went limp as the seagull had successfully broken its neck.

What came next was what bothered me the most: I expected the seagull to feast on the duckling, waiting to be proven wrong that a bird would kill out of cruelty. But it lost interest now that the duckling was dead, and it swam away casually, as the duckling's body floated to shore where the babies were playing with their shovels and buckets.

Despair washed over me. I looked over at the mother duck, who was unbothered and content with my sandwich crust. She appeared clueless that she was now one duckling short. She was watching for the wrong opportunity and had lost sight of the predator in her midst.

As I watched the mother duck sadly, I thought of the incident last night at work that weighed heavily on my mind.

"Should we make space for us to decompress and talk about what's happening?" my fellow colleague asked us anxiously during a work meeting. Another headline about a violent anti-Asian hate crime had been splashed across the media. The increase in hate crimes against our communities was a result of society blaming Asians for the COVID pandemic, but the fact was that hate crimes against Asian Americans had always been occurring. Now it had just risen to a degree to which it was undeniable. In the beginning of the pandemic, I watched a video of Sandra Oh attending a protest with others from the Asian community and allies in Oakland, California. She shouted into a megaphone, "I am proud to be Asian! I belong here!" It was almost bizarre to hear someone so well-known say that, a sentiment that was missing from my childhood. But as an adult, my heart swelled to hear the words.

"Are those Asian hate crimes still happening?" another colleague asked, confused.

I looked at her incredulously. Haven't they been happening since the Yellow Peril? Since Pearl Harbor? It struck me how if it is not portrayed in the media, society seems to pretend hate crimes don't exist.

"No, no, no . . ." Now a different colleague spoke up. "That's the media. There are no Asian hate crimes." He then turned to me. "Y'all are doing just fine with your teriyaki joints. I see everyone lined up outside your teriyaki places; you guys are making a ton of money! You guys are lawyers, doctors . . . you're all super successful."

My jaw dropped. I couldn't believe what I was hearing. It was textbook model minority myth, weaponized to refute the existence of racism against Asian Americans. "And if anti-Asian hate crimes *were* happening," he continued, "why don't y'all do something about it? Instead of just being quiet? Why don't you speak up? I haven't heard y'all say anything about it." This man had bought into the model minority myth: once again, the idea that Asians being successful in this country erased any evidence of racism.

I wanted to scream. I wanted to insult the man for revealing his lack of intelligence. I wanted to proverbially hit him below the belt and make him feel sorry. I wanted him to apologize to me. I forced myself to be momentarily silent and reflect on how to respond. I thought about my father's monk-like resilience—to let comments roll off his back, like water off a duck. Who did I want to be today? How did I want to internalize what this man was saying? Did I want to be angry? Lose control? My stomach was churning, sickened by the erasure of what the Asian American communities were experiencing while having our identities reduced to a few stereotypes.

However, my mind was clear, more than ever. I practiced my father's serenity while simultaneously tapping into my mother's gift of defiance. My mind began to work out a logical response to hopefully make this man see what was so problematic about his mindset. I took a deep breath, much like someone snorkeling and plunging back into deep waters would. I thought of the roller-coaster ride all those years ago in Korea, when my uncle had yelled, "*Heem-peh-rah!*" and I had felt more secure in my seat after I'd let go of the handlebars and moved with the motion of the ride. When faced with this ignorant man, I had to let go of control. This didn't mean I had to let go of control over myself but, above all, the situation and other people. I then truly understood that I can never control anyone other than myself.

"Actually, we're not being quiet," I began. "You're being offensive. I don't know if you've seen the several protests occurring around the country against Asian hate. And I think that just because"—I paused—"*you* think teriyaki joints are successful, that's not proof that hate crimes are not occurring. Because of the rhetoric around our former president calling COVID the 'China flu,' people are now mistakenly blaming all Asian Americans for the pandemic. Which hopefully you can see is untrue."

The man shrugged. I knew I didn't change his mind, but it didn't matter, because I also wielded my father's gift.

When I stopped blaming my mother for her shortcomings and began to heal the generational trauma, the rift that had developed over thirty years between my mother and me, I didn't know quite how to reconcile the dissonance between my identity and how society saw me. But then again, I understood the power in protecting my peace. And that was due to my discovery of newfound strength—my father's strength, his gift to me. And this was all thanks to a little story my father shared with me about a head of lettuce.

Back on Coulon Beach, I looked around desperately for something—anything. My eye caught an apple core that someone had left on the sand, and I instinctively picked it up. I quickly identified the seagull who had killed the duckling. I took careful aim and pitched the apple core as if I were in the major leagues. The apple made contact, and much to my satisfaction, the seagull went under water. But my feeling of satisfaction didn't last long as I watched the mother duck and her ducklings swim away, one duckling short.

SAH-RAHNG-HEH
(I LOVE YOU)

"Joan," my mother said, several months after the memorable Christmas when she apologized. It was finally spring again, and the cherry blossoms were in bloom once more. I was thirty-four years old and sitting on my living room couch. We were just about to hang up the phone.

"Yeah, Umma?" I answered.

"*Sah-rahng-heh.*" The words caught me off guard. *I love you.*

"I love you too." It felt foreign in my mouth, like practicing a new phrase in a different language.

It wasn't until I stopped looking at my mother through my American lens and saw her through a Korean lens that I was finally able to understand her. And I wasn't able to use my Korean lens until I embraced my Korean heritage, instead of fighting against it, something I'd felt the need to do since I was a little girl. Society had taught me that my heritage was something to hide, and I had listened. And unlike what I had readily accepted for most of my life, I know now that having multiple cultural lenses and being able to switch between them is a gift. The space between two cultural identities—the in-between space—is a gift. Because my identity does not reside on one side or the other. It remains floating between the two, ready for me to give it shape and make it my own.

Above all, I will never forget the most valuable gifts that I had inherited: my father's gift of endurance and protecting inner peace. And my mother? What else—the gift of defiance.

I didn't fully understand myself until I learned about my family, learned about Korean culture and my parents' home country. I didn't understand what strength meant until I learned about my parents' definition of strength and endurance. I didn't understand where I got my fiery passion until I learned about Korea, my country's history. This strength didn't belong to my parents. It was from my country and had been passed through my parents to me—my Kimchi Rage.

But some inheritances and generational harms are better left in the grass, like the unripe chestnuts we left on the ground in the fall seasons in front of the library. Some are better left forgotten rather than passed on.

"Mama, do you love me?" My son startled me, interrupting my thoughts. I didn't notice that he had walked into the living room where I was sitting and staring off into nothingness. His dark brown eyes looked at me expectantly but with a touch of uncertainty. His chocolate-colored hair was tousled, as if in a constant state of bed head.

"I love you more than anything," I replied without hesitation. He grinned.

ACKNOWLEDGMENTS

Thank you to my devoted husband, best friend, and soulmate, for your unwavering faith in me.

To my son, who brought me back to life. Everything I do, I do for you.

Thank you to Dori Jones Yang, who guided my dreams throughout the years. And for helping navigate this green, naive author through the industry. I am utterly grateful for your mentorship.

A special thank-you to Brooke Warner, who strengthened my craft and encouraged my book to take the form it was meant to.

To Sergeant Joyner, the first person to ever tell me that my dream of writing a book was possible.

To my other brothers in arms: Zachritz, Cam, Miller, Momsen, Gray, Rosso, Fuller, Parker, Guzman . . . the ones who had my back during my short time in the Air Force and during one of the darker times of my life. Your friendships meant more to me than you will ever know.

ABOUT THE AUTHOR

Dorothy Huynh

A national Diversity, Equity and Inclusion (DEI) conference presenter and consultant, Dr. Joan Sung has a BA in English with an emphasis in creative writing, an MA in English, and a doctorate in education. Her articles regarding Asian American voices have been published in TinyBeans.com, *Mochi Magazine*, *Memoir Magazine*, and *Writerly Magazine*. She has received a United States Air Force Medal of Achievement.

Looking for your next great read?

We can help!

Visit www.shewritespress.com/next-read
or scan the QR code below for a list
of our recommended titles.

She Writes Press is an award-winning
independent publishing company founded to
serve women writers everywhere.